Oobleck:
What Do Scientists Do?
GEMS® Teacher's Guide for Grades 4–8
(can be adapted for Grade 9)

Skills
Recording Data • Experimenting • Engineering • Critical Discussion
Communicating • Cooperating • Group Brainstorming • Decision Making
Formulating Investigable Questions • Conducting Full Inquiry

Concepts
Scientific Inquiry • Scientific Methods • Solids and Liquids • Matter
Properties • Space Probes • Models • Non-Newtonian Fluids • Suspensions

Themes
Systems and Interactions • Models and Simulations • Patterns of Change
Matter • Stability • Structure • Scale

Mathematics Strands
Logic and Language

Nature of Science and Mathematics
Scientific Community • Interdisciplinary • Cooperative Efforts
Creativity and Constraints • Theory-Based and Testable
Changing Nature of Facts and Explanations • Real-Life Applications
Science and Technology

Time
Four to five 45–60 minute periods
Two optional activities: one is a 45-60 minute period;
the other is four to six 45-60 minute periods

Original teacher's guide by
Cary I. Sneider

New GEMS® revision by
Kevin Beals and **Lincoln Bergman**

Great Explorations in Math and Science (GEMS)
Lawrence Hall of Science
University of California at Berkeley

D1159454

Lawrence Hall of Science,
University of California,
Berkeley, CA 94720-5200

Director: Elizabeth K. Stage

Illustrations
Lisa Haderlie Baker
Adria Mortellito Peterson

Photographs
Cary Sneider
Steven Dunphy

Cover Design
Lisa Haderlie Baker
Lisa Klofkorn

GEMS Staff

Director: Jacqueline Barber
Associate Director: Lincoln Bergman
Mathematics Curriculum Specialist: Jaine Kopp
GEMS Network Director: Traci Wierman
GEMS Workshop Coordinator: Laura Tucker
Staff Development Specialists: Lynn Barakos,
   Kevin Beals, Ellen Blinderman, Joëlle Clark,
   John Erickson, Karen Ostlund
Distribution Coordinator: Karen Milligan
Workshop Administrator: Terry Cort
Trial Test and Materials Manager: Cheryl Webb
Financial Assistant: Vivian Kinkead
Distribution Representative: Erica Levine
Director of Marketing/Promotion: Steven Dunphy
Publications Manager: Trudihope Schlomowitz
Editor: Florence Stone
Art Director: Lisa Haderlie Baker
Senior Artists: Carol Bevilacqua and Lisa Klofkorn
Designers: Chris Patrick Morgan, Stacey Luce
Staff Assistants: Azeen Ghorayshi, Brandon Hutchens,
   Katie Muckle

GEMS Contributing Authors: Jacqueline Barber, Katharine Barrett, Kevin Beals, Lincoln Bergman, Susan Brady, Beverly Braxton, Mary Connolly, Kevin Cuff, Linda De Lucchi, Gigi Dornfest, Jean C. Echols, John Erickson, David Glaser, Philip Gonsalves, Jan M. Goodman, Alan Gould, Catherine Halversen, Kimi Hosoume, Susan Jagoda, Jaine Kopp, Linda Lipner, Larry Malone, Rick MacPherson, Stephen Pompea, Nicole Parizeau, Cary I. Sneider, Craig Strang, Debra Sutter, Herbert Thier, Jennifer Meux White, Carolyn Willard

Previous staff members who contributed to earlier planning for, testing of, and comments on this New GEMS edition:
Associate Director: Kimi Hosoume
Network Director: Carolyn Willard
Principal Editor: Nicole Parizeau
Staff Assistants: Marcelo Alba, Kamand Keshavarz

Initial support for the origination and publication of the GEMS series was provided by the A.W. Mellon Foundation and the Carnegie Corporation of New York. Under a grant from the National Science Foundation, GEMS Leaders Workshops have been held across the country. GEMS has also received support from: Employees Community Fund of Boeing California and the Boeing Corporation; the people at Chevron USA; the Crail-Johnson Foundation; the Hewlett Packard Company; the William K. Holt Foundation; Join Hands, the Health and Safety Educational Alliance; the McDonnell-Douglas Foundation and the McDonnell-Douglas Employee's Community Fund; the Microscopy Society of America (MSA); and the Shell Oil Company Foundation. GEMS also gratefully acknowledges the contribution of word-processing equipment from Apple Computer, Inc. This support does not imply responsibility for statements or views expressed in publications of the GEMS program. For further information on GEMS leadership opportunities, or to receive a catalog and sign up for the GEMS *e-NetworkNews*, please contact GEMS.

Printed on recycled paper with soy-based inks.

ISBN: 978-0-924886-91-1

Printed on recycled paper with soy-based inks.

Note: First version published in 1985, and reprinted with revisions in 1988, 1991, 1993, 1994, 1996, 1998, 2002.

ACKNOWLEDGMENTS

Key ideas for *Oobleck* activities were contributed by Martha Constantine, Alan Friedman, Alice Spencer, and Dick Spencer. The first published reference to this activity was in "A Laboratory and Discussion Approach to High School Science Teaching" by the original author of this guide, Cary I. Sneider, in *The Physics Teacher,* January, 1971.

The term "Oobleck" is derived from the book *Bartholomew and the Oobleck* by Dr. Seuss. © 1949, Dr. Seuss Enterprises, L.P. The term is used by permission of Dr. Seuss Enterprises, L.P., and Random House, Inc.

The children's drawings that appear in this booklet were made during classes conducted by Margaret Lacrampe at Sleepy Hollow School in Orinda, California. The two drawings were originated by Chris Alonso and Mijo Brinkerhoff, and are reprinted here with permission.

Notes on the New GEMS Revision: Kevin Beals and Lincoln Bergman updated and revised this GEMS classic, in consultation with Cary I. Sneider, the original author, and as part of an overall update of the series. Special thanks to Lynn Barakos for allowing us to adapt her work on classroom inquiry for the Full Investigations activity, to John Erickson for assistance with background information on non-Newtonian fluids and other matters, to Alan Gould, who provided his astronomical expertise in the updating of information on Mars missions, to Carolyn Willard for her careful consideration of changes in light of her respect and appreciation for the educational essence and pedagogical elegance of the original *Oobleck* unit, and to Jacqueline Barber, Steven Dunphy, Kimi Hosoume, and Nicole Parizeau.

Bruce Birkett, former Professor of Physics at U.C. Berkeley, was kind enough to provide us with his scientific review of the New GEMS edition. We are indebted to him for both his scientific expertise and educational acumen. Any errors or misstatements, however, reside with GEMS and will be corrected in future editions! ■

As Oobleck once more goes to press
We wanted to again express
Our thankfulness to Dr. Seuss
Modern-day rhymester Father Goose
For his stories of wild imagination
Gentle but righteous indignation
As if such accomplishments weren't enough
He gave us a word for green, gooey stuff
We borrowed it, with all due respect
Thanks, Dr. Seuss, for naming "Oobleck!"

Original *Oobleck* author Cary I. Sneider dances on Oobleck.

CONTENTS

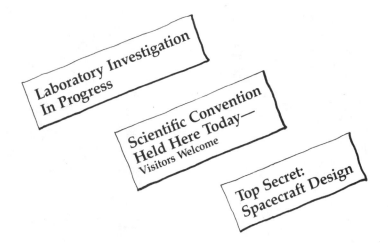

Laboratory Investigation In Progress

Scientific Convention Held Here Today— Visitors Welcome

Top Secret: Spacecraft Design

TIME FRAME

The above are guidelines to help give you a sense of how long the activities may take. The sessions may take less or more time with your class, depending on students' prior knowledge, their skills and abilities, the length of your class periods, your teaching style, and other factors. Try to build flexibility into your schedule so that you can extend the number of class sessions if necessary. In particular, the length and number of sessions for the optional "Full Investigations" activities will vary considerably, depending on your class and the parameters of their investigations.

In the late 1990s, the *GEMS Network News* print version (now the *eNetwork News*) encouraged teachers and students to see if they could "dance on Oobleck." Many responded, along with proposed explanations. For a humorous look at this subject, check out http://www.youtube.com/watch?v=f2XQ97XHjVw

For the class:

- ❏ lots of old newspapers
- ❏ 1 roll of masking tape
- ❏ 1 small squeeze bottle of green food coloring ★
- ❏ 1 extra 16-oz. box of cornstarch
- ❏ 1 measuring cup (1–4 cup capacity)
- ❏ 1 large mixing bowl or small bucket (6–8 liters)
- ❏ water
- ❏ paper towels
- ❏ markers or chalk for whiteboard or chalkboard
- ❏ whiteboard, chalkboard, or overhead projector
- ❏ overhead transparencies of Mars exploration, pages 40–44
- ❏ *(optional, but highly recommended)* selection of small wood, paper, plastic, Styrofoam, and metal items (e.g., toothpicks, popsicle sticks, plastic utensils, packing "peanuts," small paper cups, paper clips, straws, etc.)
- ❏ *(optional)* hot plate and saucepan

★ *You'll also need a medicine dropper if the food coloring is not in a squeeze bottle.*

For each team of 4–6 students:

- ❏ 1 deep plastic bowl (at least two quarts)
- ❏ 1 box of cornstarch (16 oz.)
- ❏ 1 felt-tipped marker or crayon
- ❏ 2 large sheets of paper (at least 16" x 20") or at least 10 sentence strips

Note Although pie pans may appear in older photographs for this guide, plastic bowls work well and are more durable. Plastic bowls are used in the Oobleck GEMS Kit.

For the optional Microscope Eyes activity you will also need:

For the class:

- ❏ Two clear containers filled with at least 2 cups of water. All students in the class should be able to easily see them.
- ❏ sugar
- ❏ stirrer
- ❏ spoon
- ❏ overhead transparencies of pages 52–54

For each student:

- ❏ Microscope Eyes worksheet

Quantities are based on a class size of 32 students. Please also refer to the "What You Need" and "Getting Ready" sections for each activity. Options for gathering materials for this unit:

• Some teachers prefer to gather materials needed to teach a GEMS unit themselves at local stores.

• Others prefer to purchase a ready-made GEMS Kit®.

For more information on GEMS Kits, visit the web at lhsgems.org/gemskits.html or contact GEMS.

For the optional Full Investigation activity you will also need:

For the class:
- ❑ sentence strips or sheets of paper
- ❑ tape or pushpins to attach sentence strips or sheets of paper to walls

For each team of 4–6 students:
- ❑ 1 bold felt marker.
- ❑ poster making materials

Note: The other materials needed will vary, depending on the nature of the student-originated investigations.

Listing Oobleck's properties at workshop in Jordan.

INTRODUCTION

Oobleck—even the name of this mysterious substance conjures up strange sensations. Oobleck is always a surprise. Watch it flow like a liquid, then feel its surface resist your fingers like a solid!

Since its first use in science education activities in the early 1970s, the mixture of cornstarch, water, and food coloring that we call Oobleck has been used in diverse ways by many different programs and teachers, although sometimes in a superficial way. Through many years of presentation of the GEMS unit, we've found that investigating Oobleck can be much more than having fun with a weird substance. When implemented in a coherent and carefully thought out sequence, Oobleck can be a tremendous vehicle for building conceptual understanding of key standards-based science content and inquiry.

The significant subtitle of this guide, *What Do Scientists Do?* indicates that we take advantage of the high interest and excitement that Oobleck inspires to develop important abilities related to the methods and art of scientific investigation, and to deepen student understanding of the nature of science as they experience the following:

- the excitement of exploration and discovery of a fascinating substance.

- refining ideas about the distinction between a solid and a liquid as they confront a substance that does not "follow the rules."

- the challenge of composing and refining a scientific statement.

- applying their understandings to a technological challenge, as they design spacecraft that can land on an ocean of Oobleck.

- seeing the technological innovations employed by actual Mars exploration scientists, and how they have demonstrated the nature of science in their explorations.

- reflecting on the skills and processes of being a scientist that they employed throughout the unit.

If the two optional activities are presented, students also benefit from:

- attempting to explain the properties of Oobleck by designing a model of what is going on at the molecular level.

- designing and conducting their own full inquiries to probe further questions they have about Oobleck.

As a GEMS workshop presenter prepared to present Oobleck to a group of teachers, one teacher approached and said, "Oh, I already know Oobleck. I've done it." It turned out she had done a version of Oobleck from another curriculum project. The GEMS workshop presenter suggested she participate anyway, and see what she thought. After the workshop the same teacher exclaimed, "This is so much deeper than what I've seen done with Oobleck before. I had no idea you could teach so much with it!"

One of the most appealing aspects of Oobleck is that it is not fully understood, even by scientists. This provides an authenticity to student investigations and their attempts to explain its strange properties. It also makes for a flexible unit that can be taught at a variety of grade levels. With modifications, Oobleck can be the catalyst for inspired debate with students from kindergarten through adults. In fact, it's often smilingly said that "Oobleck seeks its own level."

This well-known and widely used GEMS unit on the nature of science is often used to launch a year's science curriculum. Others use Oobleck to begin a unit on matter or a series on astronomy. The unit has always been distinguished by a learning cycle-based sequence, which includes opportunities for students to begin with an investigation, then reflect on their experiences, refine their conclusions through classroom debate and discourse, and apply what they learn in a different setting. And all of this in a relatively short and highly motivating unit!

The original GEMS unit thus provided a solid platform for this new, significantly revised 21st century edition. We've updated the information on Mars missions, to feature the two Mars Rovers. Two optional sessions have been added, *Microscope Eyes* and *Full Investigations. Microscope Eyes* is an opportunity for students to devise their own molecular/structural models for the phenomena they've explored. In *Full Investigations* students design their own investigations to pursue questions they have about Oobleck. In addition, throughout the unit we've incorporated the additional tips and nuances we've picked up over many years of teaching these activities.

Like much of active inquiry-based science, especially when intriguing substances are involved, Oobleck poses some management and clean-up issues. Class management suggestions appear throughout the guide in the step-by-step instructions. Oobleck is messy, but it is much easier to clean up than might be expected. Please see "Tips on Cleaning Up Oobleck" on pages 11 and 12 for important information.

The earlier editions of this guide included a poster about the Mars Viking mission. If you have the poster, it could also be displayed when students discuss how they acted like scientists during Activity 4.

Be on the lookout for future Mars missions. As this edition goes to press NASA's Phoenix Mars lander has just reached the red planet, and an ambitious new rover, called the Mars Science Laboratory, is scheduled to launch in 2009.

Oobleck Meets
National and State Science Content Standards

Oobleck is rich in standards-based learning and space science content. The unit addresses standards in both the K–4 and 5–8 sections of the *National Science Education Standards*. These standards are also reflected in other leading science frameworks, benchmarks, a wide range of state standards, and district guidelines.

Physical Science

• Properties of matter/changes of properties in matter/structure of matter. Objects can be described by the properties of the materials from which they are made, and those properties can be used to separate or sort a group of objects or materials. Materials can exist in different states—solid, liquid, and gas. (Note: The optional "Microscope Eyes" activity extends this content to early understandings of the microstructure of matter.)

Scientific Inquiry/Abilities and Understandings

• Identify questions that can be answered through scientific investigations; design and conduct scientific investigations; use appropriate tools/techniques to gather, analyze, and interpret data; develop descriptions, explanations, predictions, and models using evidence; think critically and logically to make relationships between evidence and explanations; recognize/analyze alternative explanations and predictions; communicate scientific procedures and explanations.

• Science advances through legitimate skepticism. Asking questions and querying other scientists' explanations is part of scientific inquiry.

Science and Technology: Abilities and Understandings

• Identify appropriate problems for technological design. Design a solution or product; implement a proposed design; evaluate completed design or product; communicate the process of technological design.

• Science and technology are reciprocal. Science helps drive technology, as it addresses questions that demand more sophisticated instruments and provides principles for better instrumentation and technique. Technology is essential to science, because it provides instruments and techniques that enable observations of objects and phenomena that are otherwise unobservable due to factors such as quantity, distance, location, size, and speed. Technology also provides tools for investigations, inquiry, and analysis.

History and Nature of Science

• Although scientists may disagree about explanations of phenomena, interpretations of data, or the value of rival theories, they do agree that questioning, response to criticism, and open communication are integral to the process of science.

Activity by Activity

Activity 1: Lab Investigation

Students form small laboratory groups to investigate Oobleck, said to be an unknown substance from a newly discovered moon in the Solar System. They learn how scientists describe the properties of a substance. During this lab session, they observe, predict, test, and investigate Oobleck and record its unique properties.

Activity 2: Scientific Convention

The class holds a "scientific convention" to discuss and analyze their findings. Discussions about the behavior of Oobleck are always animated, because its unusual nature generates controversy. Students challenge each other to define the properties of Oobleck more accurately and refine their communications skills. They also gain insight into how challenging it can be to provide enough evidence to convince an entire group to agree on a scientific statement.

Activity 3: Spacecraft Design

Your students become engineers, applying technology-related abilities and ideas, as they attempt to design a spacecraft that can land successfully on an ocean of Oobleck and then take off again without getting stuck.

Activity 4: What Scientists Do

Students become more aware of the sets of skills used by scientists that students themselves have used throughout the unit. Students learn how scientists on Mars missions faced the challenges of designing a spacecraft to land on Mars and how they explored properties of the Martian surface through the "senses" of the two Mars Rovers, Spirit and Opportunity. They learn how space scientists observed an interesting phenomenon on Mars, came up with different explanations for it, did further testing, and then came to an improved understanding.

Microscope Eyes
(optional—one class session—either before or after Activity 4)

Students pretend they have "microscope eyes" and imagine they can see what Oobleck molecules look like. They are introduced to certain scientific information about Oobleck, as a guide to come up with their own models explaining why Oobleck behaves as it does— sometimes like a liquid and sometimes like a solid. Afterward, they are introduced to explanations that have been proposed by scientists, and discuss the pros and cons of these explanations.

Full Investigations
(optional—four to six class sessions—at end of unit)

This activity maps out a series of suggested steps that provide a framework and process for successful student-centered full investigations into Oobleck. Students formulate an investigable question, design and conduct an investigation to attempt to answer this question, draw conclusions from the results, and share their conclusions with others.

Oobleck—Made for Inquiry

Oobleck has always been a splendid way for students to deepen their understanding of the nature of science and scientific inquiry. This New GEMS edition of *Oobleck* builds upon, deepens, and extends the inquiry-related opportunities for student learning. In Activities 1 and 2, Lab Investigation and Scientific Convention, students engage in and are gaining a variety of inquiry abilities and understandings, structured within the context of investigating the properties of Oobleck as they relate to solids and liquids. The *National Standards* call this guided or partial inquiry, saying: "In partial inquiries, students develop abilities and understanding of selected aspects of the inquiry process…"

Your students will of course be curious about the reasons why Oobleck behaves as it does! And they will have their own ingenious ideas. The optional Microscope Eyes activity encourages students to design their own possible molecular/structural explanations for why Oobleck behaves as it does, and to compare these with those scientists have proposed. Students are often further encouraged to pursue their ideas when they realize that scientists have many possible models, don't have a final answer, and are still investigating!

If you decide to present the optional "Microscope Eyes" activity with your students, you may want to present it after Activity 3, so students can, in Activity 4, apply their "microscope eyes" experience to the discussion of how they have acted like scientists.

As this New GEMS edition emphasizes, the *Oobleck* unit is also an excellent launching pad for the "full investigations" or "complete inquiries" recommended in the *National Standards.* What is a complete inquiry? The term is used to mean a student's ability to conduct all phases of a scientific investigation, beginning with a student-initiated question. The *National Standards* sum up the idea in this way: "In a full inquiry students begin with a question, design an investigation, gather evidence, formulate an answer to the original question, and communicate the investigative process and results." Activity 6: Full Investigations provides opportunities for students to engage in full inquiry of Oobleck. For more on inquiry, please see Resources and Background for the Teacher sections.

Language Learning and Ample Reflection

The language learning potential of this unit is rich and varied. The careful refinements of language and description that students debate as they seek to make their statements about Oobleck's behavior more accurate provide a highly motivating language arts and language acquisition activity. For English language learners, the entire series of activities, combining student-centered inquiry with discussion and reflection, makes an especially powerful language-learning vehicle. As with all GEMS guides, the unit also includes Assessment Suggestions and Resources/Literature Connections.

For all students, in order to achieve the full educational benefit of the "Oobleck experience" it is absolutely essential to allow ample time for repeated opportunities to reflect on their experience. Students should continually be encouraged to cite their evidence and explain their reasoning. It is important to ensure that there is enough discussion time for students to raise differing ideas among themselves and to generate their own conclusions after grappling with alternative explanations. Reflection upon experience is key to lasting learning.

The energy and enthusiasm generated by this mysterious substance help bring out the feelings of wonder, curiosity, and discovery that are at the heart of scientific investigation. As your students observe, experience, and reflect on Oobleck's behavior, define its properties, refine their group understanding, apply what they've learned to a technology challenge, seek explanations for why Oobleck behaves as it does, and engage in independent inquiry—they are gaining a deeper understanding of the properties of matter and the nature and practices of science. ■

The Language of Argumentation

Scientific argumentation is a key aspect of students' academic development—not only in science—but also in literacy and other domains. Science educators have increasingly paid attention to "the language of argumentation" as they examine student growth in conceptual understanding, as well as the ability of students to make explanations from evidence and to understand the essential evidence-based nature of science.

Student mastery of academic subjects is inextricably connected to the mastery of those subjects' specialized patterns of language use. The discourse and reflection in these Oobleck activities are filled with opportunities for student growth. As one study notes: "Talking offers an opportunity for conjecture, argument and challenge. In talking, learners will articulate reasons for supporting particular conceptual understandings and attempt to justify their views. Others will challenge, express doubts and present alternatives, so that a clearer conceptual understanding will emerge. In such a manner, knowledge is co-constructed by the group..." (Newton et al, 1999). If you're interested in learning more, here are a few references:

Driver, R., Newton, P., and Osborne, J. (2000). Establishing the norms of scientific argumentation in classrooms. *Science Education*, 84(3), 287-312.
Minstrell, J. and Van Zee, E. (Eds.). (2000). *Teaching in the Inquiry-based science classroom*. Washington, DC: American Association for the Advancement of Science.
Newton, P., Driver, R., and Osborne, J. (1999). The Place of Argumentation in the Pedagogy of School Science. *International Journal of Science Education*, 21(5), 553–576.
Osborne, J. F., Erduran, S., Simon, S., and Monk, M. (2001). Enhancing the Quality of Argument in School Science. *School Science Review*, 82(301), 63-70.

Students in Australia get their hands on Oobleck!

Overview

The unit opens with scientific investigation of a strange substance called Oobleck, said to come from a newly discovered moon in our Solar System. After a few minutes of free exploration, the class is introduced to the concept of properties and is focused on investigation of the properties of the strange substance. Working in small groups, they discuss and record the physical properties that they observe.

The emphasis in this first session is on direct student investigation of Oobleck. The intense curiosity and positive energy open up a learning gateway into the subsequent activities in the unit. This session sets the stage for more systematic refinement of Oobleck's properties, a challenging design application, a look at real Mars missions, and—always—more questions and investigations. From the opening exploration onward, the unit brings students a deeper understanding of what science is and what scientists do.

Learning Objectives for Activity 1

- Deepen student understanding of: properties of matter, properties of substances, and properties of solids and liquids.

- Develop student abilities in: observing, exploring using the senses, investigating, communicating, and accurately recording observations and data.

- Cultivate student awareness of what science is, what scientists do, and how students are acting like scientists.

"Discovery consists in seeing what everyone else has seen, but thinking what no one else has thought."

— Albert Szent-Györgyi, Nobel Prize winner in medicine

■ What You Need

For each team of 4–6 students:
- ❑ 1 stable, wide-topped bowl with about 1 ½ cups of Oobleck in it
- ❑ 1 work station covered with old newspapers
- ❑ 1 felt-tipped marker or crayon
- ❑ 1 large sheet of paper or about 10 sentence strips (for recording properties)

Note: Sentence strips have the later advantage of allowing the class observations about properties to be sorted in various ways.

For the class:
- ❑ 1 equipment station (see # 4 on next page). This is optional but highly recommended.
- ❑ water
- ❑ paper towels
- ❑ a piece of paper (or other familiar object) for discussion of properties
- ❑ *(optional)* dish tubs or bowls for hand rinsing

■ Getting Ready

1. **Preparation time.** If possible, **the first time** you mix Oobleck, start mixing it about two hours before class. Although it's quite possible to mix the Oobleck before class in less time, by allowing more time at first you can make any necessary adjustments more easily. In any case, you should allow at least 45 minutes to prepare the Oobleck, and to set up the work stations and the equipment station for the lab investigation.

2. **Prepare the Oobleck.** The proportions used here—4 boxes cornstarch, 6 ¾ cups (1600 ml) water, and about 15 drops of food coloring—will make enough for six teams of students to have about 1 ½ cups of Oobleck each. Keep an additional box of cornstarch on the side to thicken the mixture in case it becomes too soupy.

   a. To prepare the Oobleck, add 15 drops of green food coloring to 6 ¾ cups (1 liter 600 ml) of water in a dishtub or large mixing bowl. Slowly sprinkle in the contents of four boxes of cornstarch. Swirl and tip the bowl to level the contents.

Note: Food coloring should **not** be added after the cornstarch, because at that stage it is difficult to mix evenly. Also, adding more than the recommended amount of food coloring may cause Oobleck to temporarily stain hands.

If you have eight teams of students, you'd use about 6 boxes of cornstarch, 10 cups (2500 ml) water, and about 20 drops of food coloring.

PLEASE NOTE: *Different brands of cornstarch may require slightly different amounts of water, so you should always test the Oobleck as follows: the Oobleck should flow when you tip the bowl, and feel watery when you gently dip a finger in it, but feel like a solid when you hit it or rub your finger across the surface. If it is too thick to flow, add a little water. If it is too soupy, add a little more cornstarch. It is better to err slightly on the soupy side since some water will evaporate during class.*

On the GEMS web site at www. lhsgems.org/videos.htm there is an amusing video about mixing Oobleck, with helpful tips.

b. Mix the Oobleck with your hands (not a spoon) to ensure an even consistency. Do not try to push through the Oobleck mixture as if mixing batter, as that will prove very difficult. Instead, keep "lifting" the Oobleck from the bottom of the bowl to the top by slipping your fingers under it, until an even consistency is reached.

c. A few minutes before you plan to start the activity, mix it one more time if water has separated into a layer on top.

d. Pour about 1 ½ cups (350 ml) of Oobleck into each team's bowl. Then put the bowls aside until after you introduce the activity.

3. **Prepare work areas.** Spread several sheets of newspaper on each table where a group of students will work. If there is a rug, you may wish to spread newspaper on the floor under the edge of each table. (Oobleck can be swept up or vacuumed when it is dry, but the newspaper will make cleanup a little faster. Please see important clean up information below and on page 12.)

4. **Establish an equipment station (optional).** Students will discover the most important qualities of Oobleck by directly handling it, and by observing it in its container or while it dries on newspaper. If you wish, you can further enrich and extend the testing phase by providing an assortment of materials at an equipment station. The station could be as simple as a selection of wood, metal, and plastic items, such as coins or washers, metal and plastic spoons, scraps of wood, Styrofoam peanuts, and plastic bags.

5. **If you have dish tubs or bowls for hand rinsing, keep them handy.** It works out better for the teacher or a student to bring tubs of water to student teams rather than have students walk across the room to a centralized wash area—with Oobleck dripping off their hands. Also, to prevent waste of paper towels, you may want to keep them inaccessible and only bring them out when you want students to clean their hands.

Optional: Because students often hypothesize that temperature affects the consistency/behavior of Oobleck, some teachers provide a hotplate and saucepan at the equipment station. Of course, if you do this, make sure you've taken all necessary safety precautions and advised students on safe use.

■ Tips on Cleaning Up Oobleck

Oobleck is safe to handle and is easy to rinse off jewelry. When it dries, it can be brushed off clothes and vacuumed or swept off floors.

Oobleck can be covered with plastic wrap and refrigerated overnight, although you will likely need to add a bit more water and will definitely need to mix it a bit the next day. If kept for too long in this manner, Oobleck can become moldy. Some teachers have added a small amount of bleach to help prevent this.

Oobleck can also be left out overnight. Put the bowls of Oobleck aside until the next day so your students can see what it looks like when it dries. Reconstitute one or more of the bowls of Oobleck (by adding a little water, and mixing) for use during the scientific convention in Activity 2. Once dry, Oobleck can be dumped into compost or a wastebasket. **Do NOT pour Oobleck into the sink, as it is likely to clog the drain.** You can dispose of the newspapers that covered the work stations in the garbage.

When wet, Oobleck can be difficult to clean up, but **if allowed to dry it can be brushed off clothing and swept or vacuumed off floors.** Do not attempt to mop up a large spill—scoop up most of it first, allow it to dry, then sweep, vacuum, or wipe up the remaining Oobleck with a sponge

■ Setting the Scene

1. **Tell your students to imagine that they are a group of scientists who have been asked to investigate a strange new substance brought back from a previously unknown moon.** The moon is covered with what appear to be large green oceans, and three probes have been sent down. Contact with the first probe was lost, and what happened is unknown. The second probe is stuck on the surface, but the third probe managed to collect a sample of the ocean material.

2. **Say that the sample has now been brought back to Earth.** As scientists, they have been asked to investigate its properties.

3. **Explain that the material has been nicknamed "Oobleck" since it looks a bit like the green rain Dr. Seuss describes in his book *Bartholomew and the Oobleck*.** Show your students the bowls of Oobleck, but don't distribute them yet.

4. **Mention that preliminary studies have shown that Oobleck is safe to handle.** Tell your students that a team of chemists is trying to find out its exact composition, and their results will be revealed when their research is completed.

5. **Emphasize again that their job as scientists is to investigate the *properties* of Oobleck.** Use the following example to explain what is meant by "property of a substance" and to demonstrate the process of recording these properties. **Do not spend longer than five minutes on this exercise,** so your students will have most of the session to conduct their investigations of Oobleck.

Over the years, teachers have come up with many variations on this opening. In past editions, the space probe came back from a mystery planet "in another star system." While this connects to current telescopic discoveries of "extrasolar planets," it also fosters the misconception that travel to and from such distant systems is possible. In this edition, we've opted for the substance to come from a new moon discovered within our Solar System. Some teachers also ask the class to imagine they are on board a space ship that's near the moon, with their lab work taking place on the space ship.

One eighth grade science teacher wrote the GEMS project to describe how she introduced this unit: "I read out loud Bartholomew and the Oobleck by Dr Seuss. At first my "cool" eighth graders wanted no part of it. They were honors students; they were too old for Dr. Seuss; they were too mature! So many excuses! Yet I persisted and read to them. (They finally gave in if I would close the door so they wouldn't be embarrassed.) They loved it! And the Oobleck meant so much more to them!"

a. Hold up a piece of paper (or other object) and tell the students: "Raise your hand if you can describe this paper from what you observe, or from what you have learned by using paper." Common responses include: "It is white (or whatever color you are using)," "It is thin," "It's smooth," etc.

b. List the responses on the board, and number each one. If the students come up with statements based only on the *appearance* of paper, say: "Let's do a test." (Tear the paper.) Ask: "What can we say about paper based on this test?" Add their statements to the list.

c. Explain that the list on the board describes some of the properties of paper. A *property* of a substance is something that can be seen, heard, smelled, felt by the senses, or detected by instruments—such as microscopes, telescopes, and thermometers—that are extensions of our senses. Sometimes properties are determined through performing tests on the substance. The color, size, shape, texture, weight, hardness, odor, and sound of a substance are examples of its properties.

6. **When the group has listed at least five properties of paper, remind them that their job is to determine the properties of Oobleck.** Tell them they will soon explore the Oobleck by observing and touching it. Urge them to use all of their senses **except taste.**

Paper is just one of many objects or materials you could use to exemplify what is meant by physical properties. Many familiar objects would serve, such as a piece of chalk, a pencil, masking tape, etc.

■ Investigating Oobleck

1. **Tell students they will be working in lab teams.** Organize them into teams of four or five students each. Have each team sit around a table or desk. Have one student cover the table with newspaper.

2. **Say that after they've had a chance to investigate the Oobleck for a few minutes with just their senses, you will bring around large sheets of paper or sentence strips for each team to record the properties they discover.** At that time (if you have set up an equipment station) they may also choose from the items at the station to aid their investigation.

3. **Say that each team will have a Recorder, who will number the properties and write them down using large, clear letters.** The Recorder for each team will need to wash his or her hands. You may want to have the teams designate their Recorders at this point.

4. **Give each lab team one bowl of Oobleck. As the students investigate Oobleck, circulate from group to group encouraging them to touch the Oobleck with their fingers.**

As appropriate, if you have set up the equipment station, explain any procedures or rules for taking and returning items from and back to the station.

Investigating Oobleck is so engaging that just about the only way to get the attention of the entire class after they have begun exploring it is to remove the bowls. For this reason, going from group to group is often the best way to communicate with the class during this laboratory phase.

For example, many students think that Oobleck turns to liquid because of the heat from their hands. Point to nearby pieces of wood or plastic, or containers they might use to test that idea. Does it still act the same when a piece of wood applies the pressure? Help students learn to resolve disagreements by performing simple tests or by discussing ways to describe a property so everyone on the team agrees.

Some teachers also have students—in addition to placing stars—underline the most interesting discovery they made about Oobleck, which may or may not be the same property.

■ Recording Properties

1. **After the students have investigated Oobleck for about five minutes and discovered some of its weird properties, give each lab group a felt-tipped marker or crayon, and either sentence strips or a large sheet of paper.**

2. **Help the students start recording the properties of Oobleck.** Circulate among the groups, asking questions, such as: "What's surprising you?" "How does Oobleck behave when you press on it?" "How does the Oobleck behave when you hit it fast and hard?" "When does Oobleck behave like a solid?" "When does Oobleck behave like a liquid?" Suggest that the students test their ideas.

3. **Ask each laboratory team to put a star on their list next to the property of Oobleck they believe to be most important in explaining under what circumstances Oobleck acts as a solid or as a liquid.**

4. **Let students know that in the next class session they will discuss and debate as a class what all the lab groups have recorded as the properties of Oobleck.**

5. **You may want to end the investigation about 10 minutes before the end of the session so your students can help you clean up.**

Reminder: Please see "Tips on Cleaning Up Oobleck" on pages 11 and 12. As also noted there, you can put the bowls of Oobleck aside until the next day so students can observe it dry. Then, by mixing in a little more water, you can reconstitute one or more of the bowls of Oobleck for possible use in Activity 2.

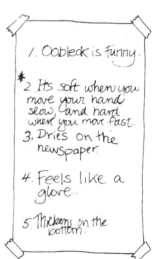

Teachers at a GEMS workshop in Jordan experience Oobleck (as Einstein looks on).

Teacher and students in Japan begin investigating Oobleck.

Overview

In this activity, the class holds a "scientific convention," similar to meetings scientists hold to focus on a particular topic or discuss findings. Their lab investigation yielded a number of different properties and observations. Now, students reflect upon, debate, and cooperatively refine their initial observations and perceived properties. Together, in a teacher-facilitated discussion, they critique and refine one statement about Oobleck at a time until there is agreement that it can be called "A Law of Oobleck."

It can be an eye-opening experience for students to discover how challenging it is to craft even one accurate statement. Students learn from other students as they consider and reconsider how best to express something they experienced. This classroom discussion stimulates the development of language and communication skills. English language learners often become so deeply involved in the discussion about Oobleck that they may overcome initial hesitancy to speak because they want to make sure everyone understands what they observed and their explanations for it.

Through this activity, students get a firsthand sense of the meticulous and exacting nature of refining scientific statements and ideas. They also learn that one of the greatest strengths of science is that it invites critique and refinement based on evidence. This kind of discussion, where students reflect on what they've experienced and learned, is an accurate reflection of what scientists actually do. Not only do scientists hold meetings to discuss and debate findings, the development of scientific knowledge is driven by the constant exchange of experiences and communications among scientists to arrive at the most accurate conclusions and expand human understanding of the natural world.

See page 21 for a sample teacher-facilitated discussion about Oobleck.

As noted in the sidebar on page 19, some teachers prefer to use terms other than "law." Also, on page 74, in the Background for the Teacher section there are definitions of scientific facts, laws, and theories that may be helpful.

The most exciting phrase in science, the one that heralds new discoveries, is not "Eureka" (I found it!) but "That's funny..."

— Isaac Asimov, author

Learning Objectives for Activity 2

- Provide students with direct experience in communicating, refining, and generalizing observations—based on evidence.

- Deepen student understanding of the nature of science—especially that scientists ask questions, query, and critique each other's findings in order to advance mutual understanding.

■ What You Need

For the class:
- ❏ 1 (or more) bowl of Oobleck, for testing ideas
- ❏ a few old newspapers
- ❏ water
- ❏ paper towels
- ❏ lists of properties from Activity 1
- ❏ chalkboard, white board, or overhead projector
- ❏ chalk, or marker for white board or projector
- ❏ 1 roll of tape

■ Getting Ready

1. **Use tape to post the lists of properties on the wall.** Optionally, you could arrange the students' chairs in a semicircle so everyone can see the lists and each other.

Note: If you are using sentence strips, gather all the strips with stars on them and display them in a single central location. You may want to arrange the rest of the sentence strips into clusters of statements organized by topic.

2. **Keep one or more bowls of Oobleck and newspaper on hand in case they are needed for further testing.**

■ Setting the Scene

1. **Explain to your students that professional scientists in most fields and disciplines come from all over the world to attend meetings called** *scientific conventions.* The topic of one meeting might be "Heart Disease," while other meetings might concern "The Planet Mars" or "Earthquake Prediction."

2. **Point out that during a convention, scientists listen to each other's experimental results and research findings and critically discuss them.** The goal of the convention is not to prove each other right or wrong, but to *arrive at the most accurate scientific statement and to state it as clearly and completely as possible.*

3. **Tell the students that they are about to hold a scientific convention on Oobleck.** The starred properties listed on the board are the scientific results they will first discuss, according to the following rules:

a. Only one property of Oobleck will be discussed at a time. First, one lab team explains or demonstrates the experiments or procedures that led to the property they starred. This is the **evidence** for their statement of the property.

b. Students who wish to agree or disagree with the property being discussed are invited to raise their hands to **explain** why. They can refer to their own experience for evidence to support their position. In doing so, students are **making explanations based on evidence**, an essential science inquiry ability.

c. Encourage students to find ways to change the wording of a property so everyone can agree on it.

d. After fully discussing a property, vote on whether or not it is really a property of Oobleck. If three-quarters of the class votes for a property, it is called a "Law of Oobleck." To illustrate what is meant in this case by a "law," tell the students that most scientists would agree that "water turns from liquid to solid below 32 degrees Fahrenheit," so it could be called a "law" of water. (Note: To be completely accurate, water turns from a liquid to a solid at 32 degrees Fahrenheit—at 1 atmosphere of pressure.)

■ Facilitating the Discussion

1. **The scientific convention can be one of the most exciting parts of the Oobleck experience because students act like scientists when they debate their views and refine their statements of properties in order to seek the most accurate scientific statement.**

2. **Your role as discussion facilitator is critical to its success.** Here are some suggestions for moderating a successful discussion:

   • The process used to arrive at a "Law of Oobleck" can take some time. Some groups start squirming in their seats after 20 minutes. Other groups are still going strong after 45 minutes. If your students are deeply involved in the discussion, you may want to continue it the following day so they can further refine their communication skills. Above all, be aware of the interest level of your class, and end the discussion when you think it is appropriate.

   • One way to maintain interest in the discussion is to break to allow one group to test a particular property of Oobleck using the bowl you saved for this purpose, demonstrating for the class, then sharing the results in a class discussion.

*Some students may be familiar with the quite elevated use of the word "Law" in science, as in the Laws of Motion, or the 2nd Law of Thermodynamics. These are general statements about physical forces and processes. Technically speaking a "law" in science has been defined as **a descriptive generalization about how some aspect of the natural world behaves under stated circumstances.** Taking Oobleck as an "aspect of the natural world" your students are indeed coming up with "descriptive generalizations" about one or more of its properties/behaviors "under stated circumstances." However, scientists themselves differ on definitions. For many, the freezing point of water would not usually be considered a "law," but a property that has been demonstrated by considerable evidence. Although the refined statements your students come up with may or may not be "laws," the use of the term adds status and motivation to their quest for scientific accuracy. There are some teachers who prefer to use terms such as "scientific fact" or "accurate statement" or "hypothesis" or "class property." The use of the term "fact" can be problematic because in everyday language it implies unchanging "truth." **Scientific fact** should be defined as in a National Academy of Sciences publication, with our emphasis on the last sentence: "If something has been observed many times by many different scientists, and no evidence has ever been found that it is not true, then it is considered to be a scientific fact. **A scientific fact is always open to being changed or eliminated if new evidence disproves it."***

While the ideal is for each group to present their starred property to the class, discussing and voting to come up with one or two "laws" may be sufficient to highlight the importance of communication and debate in science.

If you are in the unusual situation where all groups could have quick access to Oobleck, and it would not be too disruptive, then all groups could test the disputed property.

- Disagreements are starting points for fruitful discussions. After the first group has read their starred property and explained their choice, ask if anyone disagrees with that property or any part of it. If no one challenges it, ask if anyone can think of a case where that property would **not** be true.

- Once you've provoked disagreement, challenge students to find ways of *changing the wording* so everyone can agree on a statement of the property and/or pursue one or more of the options below.

3. **Here are some common ways of resolving problems that you might suggest to students to help them refine their findings.**

   a. **Add a phrase.** For example, in one class a team listed this property: "Oobleck dries out when left on paper." A student objected, saying this is not true when Oobleck is put on paper for just a few seconds. The teacher asked how to resolve the disagreement. The students added,. "for more than ten minutes." Adding such qualifiers is the essence of good scientific reporting.

   b. **Define terms.** One team listed the property: "Oobleck is sticky." When challenged to define *sticky,* they realized there are different kinds of "stickiness." After a brief debate, they changed the property to read: "Your finger will get stuck if you try to pull it out fast." A discussion like this highlights the importance of using precise terms that are agreed on by every scientist who works in a given field.

   c. **Do Another Test.** In some cases, further testing can best resolve disagreements. By keeping bowls of Oobleck on hand during the convention, you can have two or three students do the test. For example, one team proposed that contact with air made Oobleck "liquidy." Another student suggested putting Oobleck into a plastic bag where it could not touch the air. It turned out to be just as "liquidy" in the bag as it was in the bowl. After this test, the students voted not to make that particular property a "Law of Oobleck." Similarly, professional scientists sometimes report initial findings that later experiments show to be erroneous.

One teacher likes to tell students that a true sign of an intellectual—especially a scientist— is the ability to change his or her mind when presented with evidence that proves their original idea to be inaccurate.

4. **Throughout the scientific convention, ask questions and probe for student reasoning.** It is of tremendous importance that the teacher model respect and acceptance of all ideas while facilitating the discussion. One of the most important components of science learning is the chance to discuss and reflect upon an experiment or experience, both individually and as a group. This is a chance for you and your students to engage in scientific "discourse," to encounter different ideas, confront them, consider evidence, and, when possible, arrive at a new level of understanding that encompasses observations and findings more accurately.

Here is an excerpt from the scientific convention of one class:

(**T** = teacher, **S** = student).

T: Will someone from the first lab group read their most important property (the one with the star in front)?

S1: It's hard when you hit it.

T: Please explain what your group's evidence is that makes you think this is true.

S1: Well, at first it's runny, but then when you hit it, it feels hard... your hand doesn't go in.

T: Does anyone have a comment on this statement?

S2: What if you hit it lightly? See (getting a bowl to demonstrate), if I hit it slowly, my hand goes in.

S1: Slowly isn't hitting, it's something else, like just touching.

S3: It gets hard when you rub your hand over the top. You don't even have to hit it.

S4: And when you try to pick it up.

T: Can anyone suggest a word that is better than *hitting*?

S5: What about *pressing?*

S6: You'd have to say "pressing hard" or "pressing fast."

T: (to S1) Is it okay with your lab group if we change the property to read, "Oobleck feels solid when you press it hard and fast?"

S1: (after consulting with classmates) Okay, I guess that's what we meant by *hitting it.*

T: All those who agree that "Oobleck feels solid when you press it hard and fast," raise your hands... Opposed?... Abstentions?... Okay, that's 25 in favor and two opposed, so we'll call it a "Law of Oobleck." (Teacher makes change on list and circles it.) Those of you who disagree may want to think of a test to try tomorrow that may convince the rest of the class.

T: Will someone from the second group please read their most important property?...

Chris   grade 4

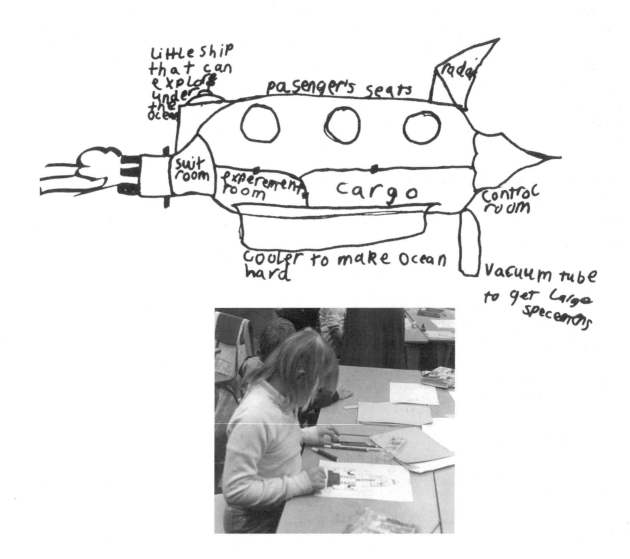

little ship
that can
explore
under
the
ocean

pasenger's seats

radar

suit
room

experement
room

Cargo

control
room

cooler to make ocean
hard

Vacuum tube
to get Large
specemens

Overview

In this activity, students are asked to apply the knowledge they've gained about Oobleck's properties to a design challenge. On paper, they design a spacecraft that is able to land on an ocean of Oobleck without sinking, collect a sample, and take off again with all passengers safely aboard—without getting stuck.

This activity serves several important purposes. It deepens student learning by motivating them to apply what they've learned so far in a new context—their close familiarity with the physical properties of Oobleck provides some of the parameters and constraints involved in the design challenge. At the same time, their creative problem-solving abilities come to the fore. Through their involvement in this challenge, they are directly engaged in activities that support the connection between science and technology. Technology, the use of scientific knowledge to propose new solutions to human problems, needs, and aspirations, and awareness of its advantages and limitations—is an important component of national and state standards.

Several "Going Further" activities are suggested as strong extensions to this design activity. Depending on your time constraints, you may want to pursue one or more of the directions suggested.

> *Truth in science can be defined as the working hypothesis best suited to open the way to the next better one.*
> *— **Konrad Lorenz**, zoologist, behaviorist, Nobel Prize in medicine*

Learning Objectives for Activity 3

- Involve students in a technological design challenge to deepen their understanding of properties and to apply that understanding in a new context.

- Contribute to student insight into the connections between science and technology.

- Foster student design and drawing abilities.

- Further develop science inquiry and language arts abilities connected to making models, critiquing, communicating, and explaining.

■ What You Need

For each student:
- ❑ 1 sheet of white paper (8 ½" x 11")
- ❑ felt-tipped markers, crayons, or colored pencils

For the whole group:
- ❑ 1 roll of masking tape

■ Getting Ready

On the board, write out any "Laws of Oobleck" that the students agreed upon in Activity 2.

■ Setting the Scene

1. **Tell students their next challenge is to design a spacecraft that is able to land on an ocean of Oobleck.** The craft has to be able to land without sinking, explore the moon, and take off again without getting stuck, with all passengers safely aboard.

2. **Explain that the moon has conditions very much like those on Earth (atmosphere, temperatures, etc.) except that the oceans are made of Oobleck.**

3. **Review the "Laws of Oobleck" that resulted from the scientific convention.** Tell the students that their designs must take these "laws" into account, along with any other observations they have made that they think are important to consider.

4. **Emphasize that the most important part of the assignment is to figure out how to build the spacecraft so it can land safely on the Oobleck and take off again.**

5. **Tell students to label those parts or features of their spacecraft that allow it to land and take off without sinking or getting stuck in the Oobleck.** As needed, they might also want to provide brief written explanatory notes for design features.

6. **Hand out paper and felt-tipped markers, crayons, or colored pencils so students can draw, color, and label their designs.** Tell students that they may work alone, or partner with one other student as a team.

7. **Let students get started on their designs.**

Do not give specific hints about how to design the spacecraft. With only the suggestions given here, students have come up with very creative engineering solutions to the Oobleck spacecraft problem. Some have designed landers with thousands of little feet that continuously press on the Oobleck so it stays solid. Others have used a hovercraft concept, high-speed cars, Oobleck dryers, or landing platforms with a detachable return shuttle.

■ Designing and Discussing Spacecraft

1. **Circulate among the students as they work, asking them how their spacecraft will land on the Oobleck and take off again.** Remind them to label their drawings.

2. **Tell each individual or team to critique their own spacecraft, listing any advantages and drawbacks to their design.**

3. **Some classes finish their drawings in one 45-minute session.** However, many classes require additional time during a second 45-minute session to complete their drawings. Some teachers assign the completion of drawings as homework.

4. **When the students are finished, allow five or ten minutes for them to circulate to view each other's drawings.**

5. **Tell everyone to be seated and ask for volunteers to explain their drawings to the class.** Invite one volunteer at a time to stand in front of the class, hold up her drawing, and explain how it will land on the Oobleck and take off again. Ask students to include in their report the advantages and drawbacks they noted in their design. Give everyone who wants to a chance to present to the group.

6. **Wrap up the presentations by asking the students which designs they think are most likely to survive the trip to and back from the Oobleck ocean.**

*Students often get carried away creating their spacecraft, including elaborate features that have little or nothing to do with landing the craft, such as laser cannons, force fields, and convertible roofs. These features are okay, **but you may have to remind your students several times that the object is to create a spacecraft that can land on and take off from an ocean of Oobleck without sinking or getting stuck.** This design challenge should be their first priority.*

■ Going Further

1. **Testing Spacecraft Ideas.** Following Activity 3, Spacecraft Design, provide students with an array of materials and fresh bowls of Oobleck to test their ideas about how to keep a spacecraft from getting stuck. You might provide different substances such as wood, metal, glass, plastic, and cardboard to see which ones float on the surface, which sink, and which ones stick to it. You could also provide springs for bouncing on the Oobleck, or rubber bands to see how much force is needed to pull a spacecraft off the surface. If your students become deeply involved in this activity, you might invite them to bring in materials from home.

2. **Three-dimensional spacecraft models.** Many teachers have extended and built upon "the Oobleck experience" by having students actually construct landing crafts from various materials, such as straws, toothpicks, balloons, meat trays, paper, styrofoam cups, packing materials, etc. The crafts must be able to land on and sit

In the GEMS unit Moons of Jupiter, for grades 4–8, students re-create Galileo's historic observations of Jupiter's moons, through viewing images provided with the guide. They also do cratering experiments, make a scale model of the Jupiter system, and go on a "grand tour" of the four main moons. In the final activity, teams of students build model settlements on one of the moons. Moons of Jupiter is an excellent companion unit to Oobleck, as are the GEMS units Earth, Moon, and Stars and Messages from Space.

upon a large tray/pan of Oobleck for five seconds, and then be able to "take off" (be lifted off) without sinking or getting stuck in the Oobleck. This is a great activity and has resulted in many ingenious models.

3. **Oobleck at Home.** Explain to the students how they can make Oobleck at home. Tell them to put one cup of water in a bowl, and add about 5 drops of food coloring. Add most of one box of cornstarch, sprinkling it in little by little, mixing until it feels like the substance they used in class. If it is too soupy, they should add a little more cornstarch. Of course, remind them about cleanup precautions and methods.

4. **Oobleck Sci-Fi:** Ask your students to make up stories about creatures who live on the moon with the green Oobleck oceans. How does Oobleck affect the weather systems? How do these creatures survive if they fall into the ocean? What do they eat? What do they look like? What are some of their social customs? How might they respond to visitors from Earth?

Some land-on-and-take-off-from-Oobleck spacecraft designs from Japan.

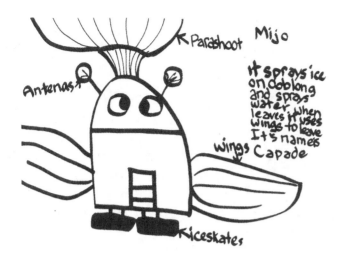

Parashoot Mijo

Antenas

It sprays ice
on oblong
and sprays
water
leaves when
wings it uses
to leave
It's name is
Capade

Wings

Iceskates

Pounding
Person

Fish

Oobleck

A green foam rubber "Oobleckian" envisioned by workshop participants in Jordan.

Scientific integrity is… a kind of utter honesty—a kind of leaning over backwards. For example, if you're doing an experiment, you should report everything that you think might make it invalid—not only what you think is right about it: other causes that could possibly explain your results… The idea is to give all of the information to help others to judge the value of your contribution; not just the information that leads to judgment in one particular direction or another.

— Richard P. Feynman, physicist and educator

Overview

Throughout the *Oobleck* unit your students have been acting as scientists. In this session, they become much more aware of this, and get a chance to think about what science is all about and what scientists actually do. In this activity, the class brainstorms the many ways they have acted as scientists during each of the activities of the unit, becoming aware of how many scientific skills they have been engaging in and are able to list.

Students compare their efforts in investigating Oobleck, debating results and designing a space ship to the work of scientists who plan and implement actual missions to Mars. Through an overhead transparency presentation, students see how Mars scientists designed a real spacecraft with clever devices to land on and explore Mars. They also are shown an example of how scientists encountered an intriguing phenomenon on Mars, came up with different explanations for it, performed further tests, and then reached agreement. Students are encouraged to keep thinking like scientists!

One of the most important ideas in current science education research is that students need to develop both science-related abilities *and* a conscious understanding of the nature of science and the ideas behind scientific inquiry. They need to be able to do science and to reflect on science as a discipline. It's also beneficial for students to reflect on *how* they've learned something, which helps them to be able to apply the process to new learning situations. The Oobleck experience is made to order for deepening of both abilities and understandings.

Learning Objectives for Activity 4

- Deepen student understanding of and insight into the nature of science and the work of scientists.

- Develop student ability to reflect on and generalize about science from their firsthand experiences and from learning about the work of other scientists (secondhand experiences).

- Provide students with information about NASA Mars missions, particularly the Mars Rover missions.

If you've presented the "Microscope Eyes" optional activity prior to Activity 4, then students will also have that experience of making models and envisioning the micro-structure of Oobleck to take into account during the brainstorm.

There are many excellent NASA-related websites that can provide you and your students with great images and information about past and current Mars missions, other missions, space science in general, as well as profiles of scientists from many backgrounds. A small sampling of these is provided in the Resources section.

This activity is a practical example of the recommendation in the National Science Education Standards that students should acquire both "abilities necessary to do science inquiry" and "understandings about science inquiry." It also exemplifies what education researchers and learning specialists call "metacognition." In its simplest sense, metacognition means "thinking about thinking." It's the awareness individuals have of their own thinking and learning processes and strategies. That awareness helps them monitor, regulate, and direct these processes and strategies toward new learning. In this case, your students are consciously reflecting on the things they did within the context of scientific inquiry (what scientists think and do). In doing so, they are more likely to recognize (and make use of) scientific modes and methods of doing and thinking the next times they encounter them. The real-world connection to the work of NASA scientists further strengthens their metacognitive understanding.

■ What You Need

❏ overhead transparencies of the Mars mission (pages 40-44)
❏ overhead projector
❏ *(optional)* LCD projector to project the transparency images directly from the Internet
❏ *(optional)* additional Mars images downloaded from the Internet

■ Getting Ready

1. **At the top of the chalkboard write three headings: LABORATORY, CONVENTION, and SPACECRAFT DESIGN.**

2. **Nature of Science Quotation.** Make an overhead of the Einstein quotation at the end of this session. You could also add other quotes on the subject, some of which appear throughout this guide.

■ Setting the Scene

1. **At this point you can announce that the research team of chemists you mentioned at the start of the first Oobleck investigation has just reported its findings on the exact composition of Oobleck.** They have revealed that Oobleck is made of cornstarch, water, and green food coloring.

2. **Remind your students that there were several parts to the Oobleck activity: a laboratory session, the scientific convention, and the spacecraft design challenge (also "microscope eyes," if you did it).** Explain to your students that during all of these activities they did many things that scientists and engineers do.

■ Students as Scientists

1. **Ask your students to describe some of the ways they behaved like scientists during the laboratory session.** List their ideas on the chalkboard under the "LABORATORY" heading. Following is a typical list: looked, touched, smelled, wrote ideas, experimented, tested ideas, talked, used instruments (plastic spoons, etc.), compared Oobleck with things we know about.

If you have done the Microscope Eyes activity, write it as a heading as well.

If students are not familiar with what engineers do and/or to make sure all students understand the term, you may want to briefly explain what an engineer does. You could say that an engineer is a person who uses science and math knowledge to solve practical, technical problems for society. Engineers design, build, and/or operate equipment, structures, and systems. There are many different kinds of engineers, including electrical, mechanical, industrial, mining, chemical, environmental, biochemical, and aeronautical engineers.

The important thing is not to stop questioning. Curiosity has its own reason for existing... I am neither especially clever nor especially gifted. I am only very, very curious.
— Albert Einstein

2. **Ask the students to list the ways they acted like scientists during the scientific convention.** List their ideas under the "CONVENTION" heading. Here is what one class listed: talked, disagreed, argued, explained our experiments, changed words, defined words, criticized, did more experiments, voted, decided if we thought something was true.

Note: If you did the Microscope Eyes activity with your students, ask how they acted like scientists during that activity as well. They might come up with a list like this: created explanations, designed models, illustrated ideas, shared models with each other, evaluated models, critiqued each others explanations, changed ideas, thought about properties of Oobleck.

3. **Ask students to list the ways they acted like engineers when they designed spacecraft to land on an ocean of Oobleck.** List their ideas under the "SPACECRAFT DESIGN" heading. They might come up with a list like this: defined a problem, came up with solutions to the problem, discussed and evaluated ideas, illustrated ideas, thought about properties of Oobleck and about how other materials behave in Oobleck, considered constraints, invented machines, changed ideas.

4. **Point out that many of the ways they acted like scientists and engineers directly reflect what professional scientists and engineers think about and do.** Tell students that, as an example of this, you are going to show them a series of overhead transparencies of the Mars Rover missions of 2004.

5. **But first, say that are going to propose a quick challenge to your students.** Say, "You designed spacecraft to land on Oobleck, taking into consideration what you knew about the fictitious moon and its surface. Mars is an actual planet, and we know many things about it, such as: it's a rocky planet, like Earth is; its atmosphere is 1% as thick as Earth's; and its gravitational pull is 38% of Earth's.

6. **Ask students—"If you were scientists designing a spacecraft to land on and explore Mars you would need to take these factors, or constraints, into consideration.** If you were to design a spacecraft that could safely land on Mars, what kinds of devices do you think might be needed?" Hold a brief discussion. [Answers will vary]

7. **Use the following notes and the overhead transparencies you prepared to present a glimpse of how scientists have addressed the challenges of real world Mars exploration.**

The purpose of this part of the activity is to draw a parallel between what scientists and engineers do and what your students have done in investigating Oobleck, conducting a scientific convention, and designing spacecraft. Sometimes groups have a hard time generating lists of ways they acted like scientists or engineers. In these situations, rather than trying to pull these responses out of them, go ahead and list how you noticed them acting as scientists and engineers.

The scientist merely explores that which exists, while the engineer creates what has never existed before.
— Theodore Von Kármán

■ Mars Exploration

Almost all of these images can be found at: http://marsrovers. jpl.nasa.gov/mission/tl_entry1. html in case you would prefer to project them from a computer rather than an overhead projector. The "blueberries" picture (#14) can be found on several sites, including: http:// marsrovers.nasa.gov/gallery/ press/opportunity/20040312a/ xpe_blueberry_b-B047R1_br.jpg

Other information: The friction also heated up the outside surface of the heat shield to as hot as the surface of the Sun (1,447 degrees Celsius, or 2,637 degrees Fahrenheit). Protected inside, the rover stayed at about room temperature.

Other information: The parachute was deployed after about four minutes and at about 30,000 feet above the surface when the spacecraft was traveling at about 1,000 miles per hour.

1. **In 2004, two vehicles without people on them, called "rovers," and named Spirit and Opportunity, landed on Mars to explore and look for evidence that there once was liquid water on Mars.** Scientists and engineers built a clever series of devices to land the Rovers safely on this rocky planet with an atmosphere 1% as thick as Earth's and with 38% of the gravitational pull as Earth's. As the two landers approached Mars, they were traveling at about 12,000 miles per hour. They were controlled by NASA scientists on Earth.

2. **In what the NASA scientists called "six minutes of terror," because they were worried that something would go wrong, the spacecraft had to be slowed down from 12,000 miles per hour to 0 in just six minutes.**

Image #1 – Heat Shield

• The friction of the heat shield in the Martian atmosphere slowed the lander down by thousands of miles per hour.

Image #2 – Parachute

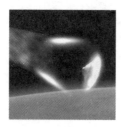

• The "supersonic parachute" was deployed. Because the Martian atmosphere is only 1% as thick as Earth's, a parachute alone could not slow it down enough.

Image #3 – Heat Shield Separating

• After 20 seconds the heat shield separated and fell off.

Image #4 – Lander on Tether

• 10 seconds later, at 20,000 feet, the lander separated from the back shell and slid down a long tether. At the end of the tether it was far enough away from the rockets and had space to inflate its airbags.

Image #5 – Three Photos of Surface

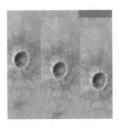

• At about 8,000 feet above the surface of Mars, with only about one minute till landing, the Rover took three photos of the surface and used its radar to figure out how high it was and how fast it was falling. It used this information to guide how it fired its rockets to slow itself down.

Image #6 – Airbags

- Airbags surrounding the lander inflated. The airbags had to be strong enough to protect the aircraft as it was landing on hard rocks.

Image #7 – Retro Rockets Fire

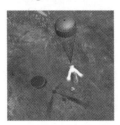

- At only one football field length above the ground, the retro rockets fired. They slowed the lander to a complete stop at about 40 feet above the ground.

Image #8 – Freefall

- 3 seconds before landing, the tether was cut and the 1,200-pound lander went into a freefall.

Image #9 – Landing

- The spacecraft bounced about 32 times up to four or five stories high! It bounced and rolled at freeway speeds for about 10 minutes then came to a complete stop.

Image #10 – Lander Unfolds

- The lander deflated and pulled in the balloons, then slowly it unfolded to reveal the Rover.

Image #11 – Mars Rover

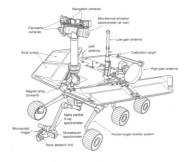

- The Rover explored the Martian surface with sensory tools to learn about its properties, much like you explored Oobleck's properties with your own senses. On its robot "arm" it had:
    - a close-up magnifier to see the texture of the rock.
    - a device that can tell what chemicals are in the rock.
    - a tool that breaks open rocks to see what they look like inside.

  It also had a panoramic camera on its "mast," and was able to travel around the Martian surface on wheels.

Image #12 – Orbiting Spacecraft

- The Rover sent information to another spaceship orbiting Mars, which then sent it back to Earth.

Image #13 – Martian Surface Photo

- This is a photo of the Martian surface that the Rover sent back to Earth.

Image #14 – "Blueberries"

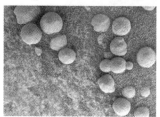

- The next example of what the scientists did is similar to the testing and exchange of ideas you did with Oobleck. The Rovers discovered interesting round mineral formations about the size of BBs that they called "blueberries." There was disagreement and debate about what they were.

3. **Ask students about these formations.** Ask, "How do you think these mineral formations might have formed? [answers will vary]

4. **Tell the class that some scientists thought they might have been formed by volcanic lava flying through the air.** Others thought they might have been formed in water—which would fit with other evidence they'd collected for the presence in the past of liquid water on Mars. Others said that the triplet formation (three balls connected in a row) shown in the photo is unlikely to have been formed by lava.

5. **Explain that Mission scientists evaluated all these ideas and decided to perform a chemical test on the "blueberries" to learn more.** The test showed that the "blueberries" matched a type of mineral (hematite) that forms in water on Earth. They decided that these minerals were probably more evidence that liquid water once existed on Mars.

Image #15 — "Spirit Celebration"

• This photograph shows NASA scientists and engineers celebrating the successful landing of Spirit, one of the Mars rovers.

■ Summing Up

1. **Explain that there have been many other missions aimed at finding out more about Mars, but never a mission where people traveled there.** Who knows, the first person to ever travel to Mars might be sitting in the classroom!

2. **Explain that science attempts to explain the physical world based on evidence and logic.** Even if most scientists agree on the correctness of an idea, they remain open to a new experiment or argument that might change their opinions. One of the greatest strengths of science is that it welcomes critique and testing of old ideas as well as the proposing of innovative new ideas, when they are supported by all available evidence, or when new evidence is gathered.

Many students are surprised that humans have never traveled to Mars!

3. **Say that because many ideas in science are based on observations and experiments over many years, they are likely not to change.** They are supported by a lot of evidence. Nevertheless, all scientific ideas are open to change and improvement based on evidence—science is an ever-changing body of knowledge. Science is a constant questioning process. Over the course of the history of science, sometimes even the most widely accepted ideas and theories have been overturned.

4. **You may want to end with one or more of the quotes on the nature of science included in this guide or a favorite of your own.** If you don't think most of these would be appropriate for your students, we at least recommend this one by Albert Einstein:

"The important thing is not to stop questioning. Curiosity has its own reason for existing... I am neither especially clever nor especially gifted. I am only very, very curious."

— Albert Einstein

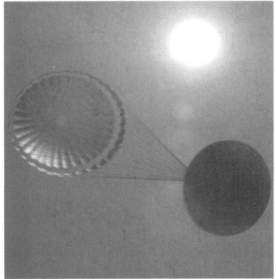

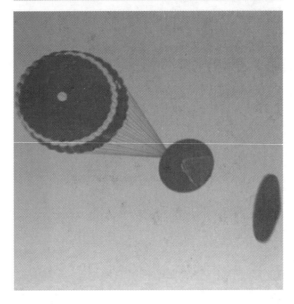

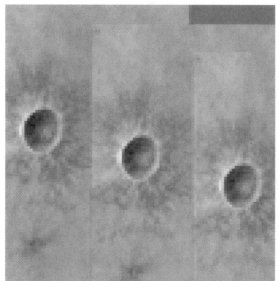

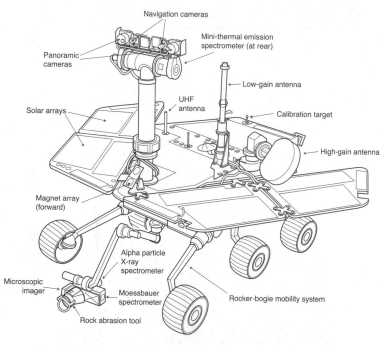

Navigation cameras

Mini-thermal emission
spectrometer (at rear)

Panoramic
cameras

Low-gain antenna

Solar arrays

UHF
antenna

Calibration target

High-gain antenna

Magnet array
(forward)

Alpha particle
X-ray
spectrometer

Microscopic
imager

Moessbauer
spectrometer

Rocker-bogie mobility system

Rock abrasion tool

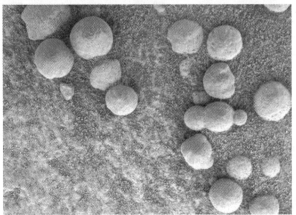

"The important thing is not to stop questioning. Curiosity has its own reason for existing... I am neither especially clever nor especially gifted. I am only very, very curious."
— *Albert Einstein*

Overview

One fascinating way to deepen and extend this unit is to ask your students to pretend they have "microscope" eyes. These eyes allow them to see/imagine what the microstructure of Oobleck might be and how this structure might account for its unusual behavior. This encourages them to think beyond the observable physical properties, to begin considering the realm of the particulate theory of matter, involving atoms and molecules, which is crucial to a later more sophisticated understanding of chemistry and physics.

Students are first introduced to some of the information about Oobleck that scientists do know. Students are told about cornstarch, what its molecules are like, and why Oobleck is considered to be a suspension. **Use your judgment as to how much to introduce— this information can be helpful to students, but too much complexity and detail can be confusing and/or cause some students to be less creative when conceiving and designing their own models.** Some teachers prefer to make only a very brief introduction.

Students use the Microscope Eyes worksheet to design their own explanations for why Oobleck behaves as it does. They are encouraged to be creative and inventive, but also to try to design models that accurately reflect their own direct observations and discoveries, and are consistent with what scientists already know about Oobleck.

As it turns out, scientists do not know precisely why Oobleck behaves as it does—sometimes like a liquid, sometimes like a solid. Emphasizing this to students helps make this thought exercise more interesting to them. Later, after students design their own models, they are introduced to three explanations proposed by scientists. They discuss the pros and cons of these alongside their own explanations.

"Microscope Eyes" does convey the idea that students should try to visualize things that are too small to see with the naked eye, as a microscope does. However, for the purposes of scientific accuracy, you may want to point out that even the most powerful light microscopes do NOT allow people to see atoms because atoms are way too small! Scanning tunneling electron microscopes do allow detection of individual atoms, but this results in a computerized image, not a direct visualization. If you wanted to introduce your students to a rapidly emerging field of science, you could discuss nanoscience and nanotechnology (a nanometer is one-billionth of a meter). Then if students are asked to visualize what things might look like and behave that are so small that not even a microscope can see them, you could ask them to use their "nanovision!"

■ What You Need

- ❑ 2 clear containers
- ❑ sugar
- ❑ cornstarch
- ❑ stirrer
- ❑ spoon
- ❑ Microscope Eyes worksheet
- ❑ overhead transparencies of pages 52–54 (cornstarch at microscopic and molecular levels/molecules with positive and negative charges/suspensions)

■ Getting Ready

1. **Fill each of the two containers with at least two cups of water.** All students in the class should be able to easily see them.

2. **Set aside the sugar, cornstarch, stirrer, spoon, and Microscope Eyes worksheet.**

3. **Prepare overhead transparencies of pages 52—54.**

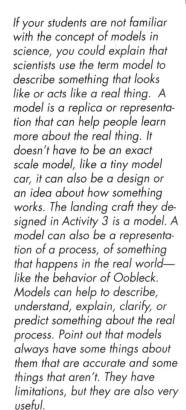

■ Setting the Context

1. **Explain to students that in this activity, they are going to imagine they have "microscope eyes."** With these eyes, they are able to see or visualize what is happening in Oobleck, at a microscopic level, as it acts like a liquid or a solid. They will draw and describe their own model of what is happening to explain why Oobleck behaves as it does.

2. **Tell your students that although scientists know many things about Oobleck, they don't know exactly why it behaves as it does.** Various models have been proposed. Say that because scientists can't fully explain the reasons for Oobleck's behavior, this provides an interesting chance for students to try to come up with their own explanations.

■ Reviewing What Scientists Know about Oobleck

1. **Tell students you'll do a quick review of some of the things scientists *do* know about Oobleck.** First, it is a mixture of cornstarch and water. Scientists, like your students, also know that Oobleck acts differently than many other substances and mixtures. It sometimes acts like a solid, and sometimes like a liquid. Many other liquids and solids and mixtures do not act this way.

If your students are not familiar with the concept of models in science, you could explain that scientists use the term model to describe something that looks like or acts like a real thing. A model is a replica or representation that can help people learn more about the real thing. It doesn't have to be an exact scale model, like a tiny model car, it can also be a design or an idea about how something works. The landing craft they designed in Activity 3 is a model. A model can also be a representation of a process, of something that happens in the real world—like the behavior of Oobleck. Models can help to describe, understand, explain, clarify, or predict something about the real process. Point out that models always have some things about them that are accurate and some things that aren't. They have limitations, but they are also very useful.

2. **Show students one of the containers of water you prepared, and tell them the clear liquid is water.** Ask them to predict what will happen if you add one spoonful of sugar and stir. If they say that it will dissolve, ask them to explain what they mean by that term. Add the sugar and stir. Can they see the sugar?

3. **If they are having trouble defining what dissolving is, explain that it is when, in a mixture, the extremely tiny particles of a substance become evenly dispersed in a liquid.** In this case, the water has broken down the sugar at the molecular level, and the sugar molecules are spread throughout the water. Tell them that when dissolving happens the result is a solution, such as the sugar water solution you just made.

4. **Show them the next container of water, and ask them to predict what will happen if you add one spoonful of cornstarch to it and stir.** Add the cornstarch and stir. Ask for their observations. Point out that it did not dissolve. Ask them what they think is going on at the microscopic level in this container.

5. **Tell them you're going to show them some illustrations representing what cornstarch looks like when magnified.** Show the overhead of cornstarch pieces, and read the statement:

• The pieces of cornstarch are sort of spherical in shape (roundish).

Tell students this is what tiny pieces of cornstarch look like at a microscopic level.

6. **Now, tell them you'll show a drawing representing cornstarch at an even smaller level—a molecular level.** Show the overhead of molecules in the cornstarch, and read the statement:

• Pieces of cornstarch are made up of many starch molecules. Starch molecules are in the shape of long chains.

7. **Tell them the lines in the drawing represent the starch molecules, which are what the roundish pieces of cornstarch are made up of, so they are much smaller than the pieces.** Explain that all matter, including Oobleck, is made up of tiny particles or building blocks called molecules that are much too small to see.

8. **Show the overhead of a water molecule with positive and negative symbols, and read the statement:**

• The molecule has electrical charges. Parts have a negative electrical charge and parts have a positive electrical charge.

Tell students that negative and positive charges are attracted to each other.

*Scientists call Oobleck and some other substances "non-Newtonian fluids" because they do not act in the way that Isaac Newton's ideas correctly predict for most fluids. Oobleck and some other substances are exceptions to the rule. When you push your finger hard into a Newtonian fluid, such as water, for example, it does not feel like a solid. Substances that change in viscosity due to shear or stress (as when Oobleck is pressed and becomes more viscous) are called non-Newtonian. To make "matters" more complex, there are also non-Newtonian fluids that become **less** viscous due to shear or stress, such as shampoo and ketchup. See Background for Teachers at the back of this guide for more information*

If the idea of electrical charge is completely new to your students, you may want to demonstrate by doing a balloon demonstration. You could rub a balloon on a piece of flannel or a sweater, and show how the static electricity created makes the balloon stick to the wall. For a nice demonstration of the opposite charges involved that account for the attraction of the balloon to the wall, see the simulation provided at: http://phet.colorado.edu/new/simulations/sims.php?sim=Balloons_and_Static_Electricity

9. **Explain that the sugar breaks down into molecules that spread evenly through the water.** But the cornstarch does **not** dissolve in water—it does not break down to the molecular level. It remains at the level of the roundish shapes, which are very small, but not anywhere near as small as the molecules.

10. **Show the overhead of a suspension and read the statement:**

   • This is muddy water. It is a suspension of dirt in water.

11. **Say that Oobleck is a suspension of cornstarch in water.** It is not a solution. In a solution particles are dissolved in the liquid. In a suspension the pieces are suspended in the water.

■ Using Microscope Eyes

1. **Tell students that this information from other scientists is just to provide them with a basis to get started with their own ideas.** Remind them they also have lots of things they already know about the properties and behavior of Oobleck from their own observations and tests.

2. **Say that their mission is to continue acting like scientists and use their microscope eyes to come up with their own explanations for Oobleck's strange ways.** They should draw and describe how Oobleck's structure at a microscopic and/or even smaller level—as they think it might be—could explain why it behaves as it does, sometimes like a solid and sometimes like a liquid. They should imagine they can see the pieces and/or molecules of cornstarch and water, and visualize how they might act when being poured, when being pushed or pulled, or during some other action students conducted.

3. **Tell them their explanations can be very creative, but need to be consistent with what is known about Oobleck.** This includes the evidence they have found through testing, as well as what other scientists have figured out. Tell them to keep their models realistic—using atoms and molecules or other scientific ideas—not things like "little people" or other imaginary creatures.

4. **Show the overhead of the Microscope Eyes worksheet.** Show them where they will draw their own ideas of what is going on in "liquid" and "solid" Oobleck at the microscopic or smaller level. Show them where they will write one or more paragraphs explaining their ideas.

5. **Explain that because scientists do not know exactly why Oobleck behaves as it does, this is an assignment in which they cannot be "wrong"** (as long as their model is in line with what we already know about Oobleck).

Some teachers have students finish the worksheets as homework.

6. **Hand out copies of the Microscope Eyes worksheet to each student.** Remind them to write their names on them. Give them plenty of time to work on their drawings and explanations.

7. **When they have finished, encourage some students to share their explanations with the class.**

■ Sharing Explanations from Other Scientists

Note: Don't share these proposed explanations with the students until they have finished their worksheets.

1. **Tell students other scientists have come up with explanations for Oobleck's behavior too. You will summarize three explanations.** Emphasize that these are not the "right" answers—they are three proposed explanations. There is not yet enough evidence to know which might be the most accurate.

2. **Discuss the Sand in Water Model.** Explain that in this model, the starch pieces in Oobleck are compared to sand and water in a plastic squeeze bottle, even though the pieces of cornstarch are much smaller than pieces of sand.

   The grains of sand are packed closely together, with a little water in between some—but not all—of them. The surface tension of the water does not allow all of the spaces between the grains to be filled with water. Squeezing the bottle *gently* forces the grains of sand to slide against each other, increasing the spacing between some of the grains, and allowing more water to fill the spaces. The more gently you squeeze, the more time there is for the water to fill the spaces between the grains and provide lubrication so they will slide against each other, and flow. But when the bottle is squeezed quickly, there is not enough water between the spaces to start with, and friction between the grains of sand resists the flow.

Stress that much remains to be learned about substances like Oobleck ("non-Newtonian" fluids, if you introduced the term). It's often of great interest to students that scientists don't know the "answers" to many things and debate conflicting ideas. It also helps deepen understanding of scientific inquiry itself—as a constant process of questioning and investigating.

3. **Discuss the Long Chains Model.** Tell students that this model bases the behavior of Oobleck on the *long chain shape* of starch molecules. According to this model, when a mixture of cornstarch and water is pushed hard against and compressed, the chains are stretched. But they are stretched in a direction that is at *right angles* to the direction of compression, so the long molecules get in the way. The molecules become "tangled," so they are not able to slide easily against each other. This makes the substance feel like a solid.

4. **Discuss the Electric Charge Model.** This model suggests that the particles in Oobleck acquire an electrical charge as they rub together. The faster they are rubbed, the more electrical attraction is created between the particles, which makes the Oobleck more viscous. A strong push or compression creates more electrical attraction, so the particles hold together more, and the substance feels like a solid.

5. **You may want to give your students time to critique both their own models and the three just presented, discussing the strengths and weaknesses of each.**

6. **You could end the activity with a statement about how difficult it is to infer what is really happening at a molecular level, based only on observable properties.** You could add that since there is no conclusive explanation as to why Oobleck and certain other substances behave as they do, a scientist of the future— perhaps one of your students—might discover more evidence to support one of these explanations, or a combination of them, or come up with a new explanation that fits the evidence better.

"Microscope Eyes"

Imagine you have microscope eyes. You can either see what those little round cornstarch pieces are doing or you can look at an even smaller level and see what the long charged molecules are doing. Draw what you think may be happening and write your explanation below.

Oobleck when liquid	Oobleck when solid

Explanation: _____

_____

_____

_____

_____

_____

_____

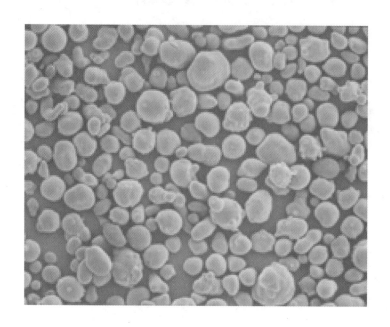

Starch

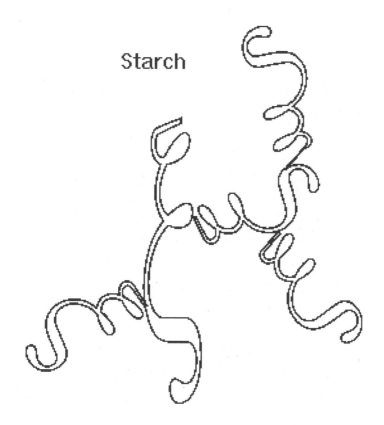

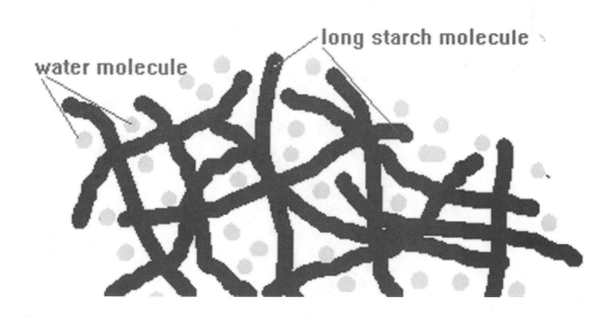

water molecule

long starch molecule

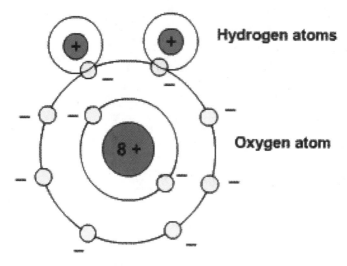

More positive charges

Hydrogen atoms

Oxygen atom

More negative charges

"Inquiry into authentic questions generated from student experiences is the central strategy for teaching science... In a full inquiry students begin with a question, design an investigation, gather evidence, formulate an answer to the original question, and communicate the investigative process and results."

– National Science Education Standards

Overview

Throughout the *Oobleck* unit your students engage in and reflect on things scientists do. They explore natural phenomena, record observations, exchange, debate, and refine their ideas, and design technology based on their findings. These are all aspects of scientific inquiry. If you have the time, and depending on your students' experience, you can crown this unit by encouraging your students to engage in the wide range of abilities and understandings that come into play when designing and carrying out a full investigation. This process includes: formulating a question about the natural world that is able to be investigated; designing and conducting an investigation to answer/learn more about this question; closely observing and describing what happens; drawing conclusions from the results; and sharing findings with other scientists.

The fascinating substance called Oobleck generates lots of questions! Because it's a safe substance, students can investigate many of these questions. This provides a wonderful opportunity for students to continue acting as scientists by launching full investigations into their own questions. However, conducting such investigations can be challenging. Depending on your students' prior experience, there are many junctures where teacher guidance is crucial. Students often need help understanding and formulating "investigable questions." It can be challenging to keep the investigations focused on relevant content. Nonetheless, engaging students in this process is well worth the time and effort!

There are many forms inquiry can take. On the following pages, we have provided one suggested sequence that may help pinpoint some pitfalls and provide a general sense of how a student investigation could proceed. However, some of our suggestions may not apply to your situation. You may already have developed strategies that work well for you and your students. That's fine!

> The outcome of any serious research can only be to make two questions grow where only one grew before.
>
> — *Thorstein Veblen,* author and social scientist

Please note that to provide students with an experience of the full inquiry process requires a fairly substantial time commitment. Depending on various factors, we estimate this will take at least three and as many as six 45-60 minute classroom sessions.

Because it is optional and intended solely to serve as flexible and general guidelines, this activity is not written in the standard session-by-session format. Instead it is an overview and outline of one possible classroom-based investigation approach and process. Some of the "phases" may be quite brief and others may take one or more class sessions, depending on the task, the age and experience of the students, your teaching style, etc. Each phase begins with a brief rationale.

■ What You Need

- ❑ cornstarch, water, and food coloring to make more Oobleck.
- ❑ sentence strips of sheets of paper.
- ❑ 1 bold felt marker per team of four
- ❑ tape or push pins to attach sentence strips or sheets of paper to walls.
- ❑ poster making materials.
- ❑ materials needed for student investigations (these will vary)

■ Getting Ready

Cornstarch

(a)

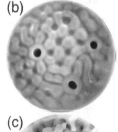

(b)

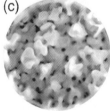

(c)

1. Clear your calendar!

2. Familiarize yourself with the approach outlined below, or consult other guidelines for student investigations.

3. Gather needed materials.

This is a top view of a vibrated layer of a suspension of cornstarch in water, at three differing accelerations and frequencies. The article is entitled "Persistent Holes in a Fluid" and appeared in *Physical Review Letters*, Volume 92, Number 18, May 2004. The authors are from the Center for Nonlinear Dynamics at the University of Texas at Austin and are: Florian S. Merkt, Robert D. Deegan, Daniel I. Goldman, Erin C. Rericha, and Harry L. Sweeney.

■ Phase 1—Generating Questions (about Oobleck)

This phase is an initial brainstorm of questions about Oobleck to get students started in their investigation process. Here's one suggestion:

1. **Tell students that over the next series of sessions, they will get to design and conduct their own scientific investigations of Oobleck based on their own questions.**

2. **Organize students into small groups, and ask them to come up with questions they have and things they still wonder about Oobleck.** They can start the process by writing down questions and wonderings individually on scratch paper. Then they should share out their questions with their group.

3. **Tell each group to write each of their top three or four questions sideways on a separate sheet of paper or on a sentence strip.** Using bold felt markers and large lettering, they should write only one question per sheet, then post them in front of the room. Explain that the reason for this is that later the class will sort the questions in various ways, so they need to be able to be moved around, and able to be read from across the room.

■ Phase 2—Focusing Investigation Ideas

In order for your students' investigations to be rich in both content and process, it can be useful to group their questions into conceptual categories. This helps prevent students from setting up an investigation only "because it would be cool," and instead focuses them on how their investigation might advance their understanding of the subject matter. This is also a chance for you to begin helping students refine the questions or generate more questions focused on a particular topic.

1. **List conceptual categories on board.** Point out the topical categories you've listed and explain that scientists often group their questions to help make sense of their investigations. Say these are some general ideas in science that Oobleck investigations could help us understand.

2. **Organize questions by conceptual categories.** Have the class help you organize their questions by category to help set a context for their investigations. Depending on the experience of your class, this will be more or less teacher-directed. Some investigation ideas that "flow" from these categories are described under the next phase. The main idea is to begin helping students connect investigation questions to big ideas in science. You and your class may come up with different topical areas to investigate that relate to Oobleck Again, that's fine!

Note: *Categories should not be materials-based, i.e., involving food coloring, etc., but rather conceptually-based, i.e., temperature effects.*

The exact categorization of questions is less important than having students think about how their questions relate to scientific understandings. You could also create a "Miscellaneous" category for questions that don't fit exactly into specific science topics.

- **Comparing and Contrasting Properties of Solids and Liquids**

- **Temperature Effects**

- **Proportions of Ingredients**

- **Viscosity-How a Substance Flows**

- **Practical Uses for Substances**

It can be challenging for students to generate questions that have relevant science content and are practical in the classroom setting. Students often come up with questions that are just for fun, require impractical materials or procedures, or can be looked up easily. Questions that are "look-up-able" or Research Questions ("How is cornstarch made?" or "What is cornstarch made of?") could be saved for later searches in books or on the Internet.

Asking students to come up with their own guidelines about what kinds of questions are able to be investigated gets them thinking about it and helps them better understand any additional guidelines you may add. A sample reminder sheet is provided at the end of this outline.

You may want to spend some time explaining why it is that "what-happens-if," "comparison" and "measuring" questions are usually investigable in the classroom setting and with time restraints, while the "why" and "how" questions are not, especially not in a single investigation. "How and why" questions can sometimes be analyzed and broken down into some aspect that can be investigated, or they can be set aside for later discussion. See Background for the Teacher in this guide and/or the GEMS Dry Ice Investigations unit for more on this.

■ Phase 3—Sorting Questions

1. Explain purpose for sorting questions. Tell students they will now think about what **types** of questions are best suited for classroom investigations. Explain that some questions are better answered by looking them up—doing that kind of research. Some questions are more able to be directly investigated in the classroom.

2. Students discuss what makes a question investigable and sort questions. Tell groups of students they will first discuss what makes a question good for investigating. Have them write down some questions from the posted categories that they think are investigable and some that they think are not. Ask them to try to come up with guidelines for choosing questions, or ways to change them so they become more able to be investigated in the classroom. After several minutes, ask students to share some of their ideas and record them on a class chart.

3. Introduce ideas about investigable questions. Tell students that the kinds of questions that are best suited for classroom investigation need to be small enough to be answerable in a reasonable amount of time and have an observable result that can provide some evidence to answer their question. "What happens if," "comparison" and "measuring" questions tend to be able to be investigated in the classroom setting.

For example, the question of "What would happen if you took some Oobleck to the Moon?" is very interesting, but not one that can be answered given the constraints of their classroom. Explain that "How" or "Why" questions are also interesting questions to ask, but they often can be too complex to find an answer through a firsthand investigation. "Why does Oobleck behave the way it does" is also a perfectly good question, but it doesn't lend itself to an investigation that they can observe something about. (If you have time for students to do research into some of their questions, you can have them select some "How" or "Why" questions for further research.)

4. Introduce materials and safety guidelines for your classroom. Display the Class Guidelines sheet and point out that there are some other guidelines you need to tell them about (materials and safety) and explain the reasons for the rules in your particular classroom. (You may need to adjust our sample sheet in order to fit your classroom situation).

Class Guidelines for Our Investigations

1. **The investigation is safe for students to do.**
2. **The question is of interest to the investigator.**
3. **The materials needed are easy to get, inexpensive, and/or already available in the classroom.**
4. **The question is important (or relevant) to understanding the properties of Oobleck and/or big ideas of science.**
5. **The question isn't too big—it can be answered by just one investigation and within one class period.**
6. **The investigation is based on a "what-happens-if," "comparison," or "measuring" question, probably not a "why" or 'how" question.**
7. **The question isn't a "look-up-able" research question.**
8. **The question can be answered/learned more about by something you can do in this classroom.**

5. Students revise their questions. Have students now meet in their investigation groups to discuss whether their question is investigable as written, or if they need to revise it. Circulate among groups and provide guidance for how to re-word or modify their question so it can be investigated within the constraints you have discussed.

Note: Making sure that students have a question that is challenging— yet reasonable in scope—is key to their success in designing their own investigations. If you see that groups are struggling with revising their questions, you may need to provide individual assistance to help them write an investigable question.

Feel free to adapt or substitute your own guidelines. For example, if students can have more than one class period for the physical investigation, then Guideline #5 can be adjusted.

As you go through each of the guidelines, you may want to ask students to help you find examples among the posted questions that fit and don't fit the guideline.

■ Some Investigation Ideas

Using the same sample categories as in Phase 2, here are possible ideas for investigations. Regardless of the categories, these ideas may assist you in helping students devise and revise their own investigations. These are just suggestions. Never underestimate the curiosity and creativity of your students. They are likely to come up with some very interesting investigations themselves. GEMS would love to hear about their work!

• Comparing and Contrasting Properties of Solids and Liquids

Compare the properties of Oobleck with the properties of other substances, such as slime, snow, hair gel, oil, or other safe substances that pose intriguing differences or similarities. Rather than doing only a general comparison, students could focus on a particular attribute and devise tests and procedures to compare and contrast the substances in that regard. Students could also hypothesize comparative "microscope eyes" models of molecular structures or other characteristics that might explain the differences or similarities.

• Temperature Effects

Students could investigate the effects of temperature on the behavior and properties of Oobleck. Does the warming or cooling of Oobleck affect its properties? How do the properties of Oobleck when warmed or cooled compare to those of another substance when warmed or cooled?

• Proportions of Ingredients

As students now know, Oobleck is a mixture of cornstarch and water. Do the proportions of these ingredients affect the properties? What would happen if one were to add more cornstarch? More water? What is the smallest amount of water that can be added that still allows liquid-like properties to be exhibited?

• Viscosity—How a Substance Flows

Students could test the relative viscosity of a number of other substances. Are there others, like Oobleck, in which they can detect a change in viscosity NOT caused by adding other ingredients or a temperature change? Is the viscosity of different substances affected by agitation, temperature, or time? Is viscosity related to density? Some suggested substances to investigate include: ketchup, wet sand, hand cream, shampoo, mayonnaise, gelatin, paint, toothpaste, honey, mud, oil, water, grease, yogurt, fruit juice concentrates.

■ Phase 4—Forming "Interest Groups"

For classroom investigation situations, groups of three to four students are often preferable. It's a balance between having enough minds for exchange about the challenge, but not so many that individual students get left out. Groups of three are often able to delve more deeply into an investigation than groups of two or individual students. For stimulating, content-rich investigations, it's important for students to be interested in the question they are investigating. The following process is one way to give students a chance to choose investigation groups, based on their interest in different categories of questions.

1. Post the questions around the room, sorted by the topical categories. Have students walk around the room looking at the questions posted under each category.

2. After looking at all the categories, tell students to return to the category with the question that most interests them, and remain there.

3. Tell them to discuss which questions interest them and why with other students who have gathered around the same category.

4. If necessary, help larger groups subdivide further to form groups of three or four students who are interested in investigating the same question.

■ Phase 5—Designing the Investigation

Although students often prefer to jump right into their investigations, it's very important that they spend time thinking about, discussing, and planning their investigations to avoid carelessness and to gain a better understanding of the process. You may want to come up with a more structured format to ensure that student groups make clear plans, such as a scaffolded worksheet.

1. Tell students they will now meet with their investigation group and make a preliminary plan. Say they should be sure to include:

   a. The question they plan to investigate.

   b. The materials they need to begin the investigation.

   c. The first steps for the investigation.

   d. How the question will help them understand more about substances like Oobleck and/or Why they want to know the answer to the question.

2. Collect their initial plans and materials lists. Tell students you will look over their plans and that they will revise them based on your feedback.

■ Phase 6—Getting Teacher/Peer Feedback

This is an opportunity for the teacher to see what the students are planning, and help redirect them or raise issues for their consideration as necessary. It also provides an idea of what materials may be needed. Explain any limitations on the availability of materials. If there is time, and depending on class experience, consider facilitating a peer review process.

In a systematic investigation, you make a plan, decide on the conditions, follow the plan, and then carefully observe and record what happens over time. In an experiment, you make a comparison between two (or more) situations, keeping all things the same except one, and then carefully observe and record what happens. See Background for the Teacher in this guide for more on scientific methods, and see the GEMS guide Dry Ice Investigations for more on these subjects, and some structured student sheets for planning and conducting systematic investigations and experiments.

1. Provide written or oral feedback to each small group to help them refine their questions and procedures and begin planning their investigations. Students can also give constructive feedback to their peers about their plans. by exchanging plans among each other.

2. As appropriate, ask student groups questions about the design of their investigation. Depending on the level and experience of your students, and the nature of their investigations, this could involve making sure each student has a role in the group, or assisting students in making sure their plan for observation is a systematic one, or helping students consider variables and whether or not their investigation is a "fair test."

3. Before students conduct their investigations, make sure their plans include how to keep track of the results. Have them discuss and decide on the method or methods they will use to record observations and measurements. As feasible, allow for groups to make any other necessary modifications to their designs before they begin the investigations.

■ Phase 7—Conducting the Investigation

The more involved the teacher can be in asking questions to help guide investigations and deepen thinking, the more successful student investigations will tend to be.

1. Facilitate small group investigations. Provide materials to groups and circulate to respond to questions that arise as students begin their investigations.

2. Encourage students to jot down questions and observations even though they may not seem relevant at the time. Ask guiding or probing questions to help students make sense of their observations and relate what they are observing/finding out to big ideas about science.

3. Build in opportunities for discourse and communication between groups about the investigation process as well as their preliminary findings, Have groups meet to share and discuss their results.

Questions to Help Students Identify Variables and Controls

- What comparisons can you make in the investigation?
- Is it a fair test? (are variables controlled as much as possible?)
- Are there any hidden variables that may be contributing to the results?
- What kind of evidence will you use to support your conclusions?

Questions to Help Students Represent their Data

- What are the predicted outcomes of the investigation?
- How will you organize this information?
- Can you quantify your results, i.e. what will you measure?
- How will you represent the data?
- Can you think of graphs that can be used to add meaning to your data?
- Can you use a graphic or picture to help present your findings?
- Are there any patterns you can identify from your data? How will you show them to others?

If there is time, you may want to allow for another investigation phase at this point—if, for example—results are not conclusive, if students have thought of a better method, if their question has changed, etc..

■ Phase 8—Group Sharing of Results

It's important for students to share their procedures and conclusions—their successes and problems. Students can learn a lot from each other about the process of conducting an investigation, and about its science content. The poster session format recommended here helps avoid the tedium that can result when every group takes a turn sharing in front of the class. It also models an authentic format scientists use and provides more opportunity for discourse between the students.

1. Assign each team to make a poster representing their investigation to share with others. The posters should include:

   - The question they investigated.
   - A description and illustration of their procedure.
   - The results of their investigation.
   - What conclusions they draw from the evidence they found or What they have learned about the big idea their question addressed.
   - What they would do differently if they were to conduct the investigation again.
   - What further questions they have about the topic.

2. Each team member will spend some time explaining their investigation to others during the poster session. Give them time to help prepare each other for this role.

3. Have each group assign one member to be the first to stand near the poster to respond to questions or comments other students have. The other members of the group can circulate, looking at and asking questions about other posters.

4. At your signal, a different member of each group becomes the explainer at their poster, and the person who was there gets a chance to circulate. Rotate students at five- to ten-minute intervals so everyone has a chance to see most of the posters.

■ Phase 9—Content Synthesis/Bringing It Together

During the poster session or other sharing of results, peer teaching is bound to happen. Still, it's very important for the teacher to help tie the investigations together, emphasize underlying connections, make generalizations about science concepts, and about what scientists do. Making this synthesis is often overlooked or skipped due to lack of time, but it is a very important part of the entire process. Having an overview of all the separate investigations deepens students' conceptual understanding. As appropriate, it can connect to relevant standards. It also builds student awareness that science is not just about "right answers," and that—even when questions may be similar there are many pathways of investigation. In turn, this can help students gain insight into a more sophisticated, expert, and complex understanding of the nature of science and the diversity of scientific investigation.

1. Encourage group interaction and questions about each other's findings. Ask questions to help them reflect on the decisions they made and what they might now do differently.

2. Help point out individual discoveries and make connections between different investigation group results and big ideas in science.

3. Facilitate group awareness of their progress toward deeper conceptual understanding. Point out patterns and connections between investigations.

4. Acknowledge further questions that have been raised by the investigations and the possible directions for subsequent investigations.

Some Questions to Help Build Larger Conceptual Understanding

• What has the new knowledge from your investigation and those of your classmates contributed to your understanding of science?

• Are there any connections between what you've learned and things in your daily life or real world problems?

• How is your investigation related to a larger field of study? (life science, earth science, chemistry, physics, etc.)

• Can you relate your investigation to any unifying themes we've studied in science?

Class Guidelines for Our Investigations

1. The investigation is safe for students to do.

2. The question is of interest to the investigator.

3. The materials needed are easy to get, inexpensive, and/or already available in the classroom.

4. The question is important (or relevant) to understanding the properties of Oobleck and/or big ideas of science.

5. The question isn't too big—it can be answered by just one investigation and within one class period.

6. The investigation is based on a "what-happens-if," "comparison," or "measuring" question, probably not a "why" or 'how" question.

7. The question isn't a "look-up-able" research question.

8. The question can be answered/learned more about by something you can do in this classroom.

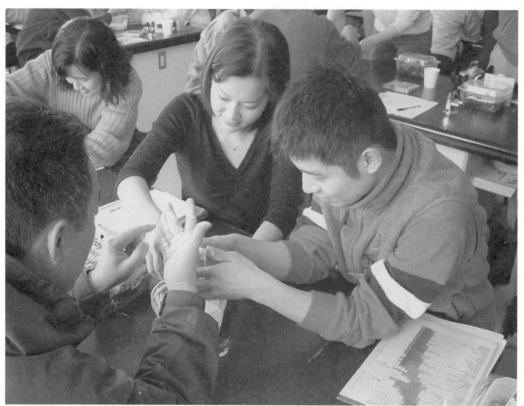

Teachers at a GEMS Workshop in Japan begin investigating Oobleck.

Teachers at a Lawrence Hall of Science workshop list Oobleck's characteristics.

Inquiry

The *National Science Education Standards* emphasize: "Inquiry into authentic questions generated from student experiences is the central strategy for teaching science. Teachers focus inquiry predominantly on real phenomena, in classrooms, outdoors, or in laboratory settings, where students are given investigations or guided toward fashioning investigations that are demanding but within their capabilities." A large number of state standards also emphasize the role of inquiry—of student ability to engage in scientific investigation and to deepen their understanding of the nature of science. The *Oobleck* unit fits these recommendations perfectly.

What is inquiry? Among many excellent examples and descriptions in the standards, the following summary stands out:

> Scientific inquiry refers to the diverse ways in which scientists study the natural world and propose explanations based on the evidence derived from their work. Inquiry also refers to the activities of students in which they develop knowledge and understanding of scientific ideas, as well as an understanding of how scientists study the natural world.

> Inquiry is a multifaceted activity that involves making observations; posing questions; examining books and other sources of information to see what is already known; planning investigations; reviewing what is already known in light of experimental evidence; using tools to gather, analyze, and interpret data; proposing answers, explanations, and predictions; and communicating the results. Inquiry requires identification of assumptions, use of critical and logical thinking, and consideration of alternative explanations. Students will engage in selected aspects of inquiry as they learn the scientific way of knowing the natural world, but they also should develop the capacity to conduct complete inquiries.

It's also important to emphasize, as the *National Standards* do, that there is no single "scientific method." In the past, many students (including most of us who now teaching science!) learned about *"The* Scientific Method." While described in slightly different ways by different teachers over time, students have generally been taught that there is a rigid, linear, step-by-step process that scientists use to find out about the natural world. This misrepresents science. (See pages 121 and 144 of the *National Science Education Standards.)*

In fact, scientists use a variety of scientific methods (note the plural). These scientific methods, perhaps better described as scientific inquiry methods, provide a repertoire of strategies that can be brought to bear in a logical progression to find out more about a situation. Many people are surprised to learn that scientists don't just conduct controlled experiments (a comparison between two situations that are alike in all ways but one), but also, when appropriate, conduct systematic observations (observing a situation with planned conditions over time) or combine a variety of other approaches, depending on the circumstances.

Although the classic scientific method sequence (beginning with question, hypothesis, experimental design, etc.) does represent a summary of key phases of a scientific investigation, it is not uncommon for a scientist to go back and forth between two phases (or inquiry methods) before proceeding to the next. So, for instance, a scientist rarely arrives at a question without having had the opportunity to first explore and observe the subject of study. Often a scientist will refine a preliminary question by again exploring with materials. Likewise, meaningful hypotheses come from having had some firsthand experience interacting with the situation. In addition, designing an experiment is nearly always preceded by running some pilot studies, in order to try out and refine procedures, identify variables, devise ways to control variables, and come up with ways to measure the test variable.

What was once called, "The Scientific Method," is now called the inquiry process. The process of inquiry is a flexible and dynamic process that includes more than just conducting controlled experiments.

Helping Students Move Beyond Natural Inquiry

Children inquire naturally. They are in fact experts at the process of exploration and rarely need guidance in inquiring in this free form way. However, moving to more systematic ways of inquiring, such as conducting a systematic observation or a controlled experiment, is something that needs to be learned and usually requires a fair amount of guidance. The *National Standards* call for students to be given opportunities to engage in partial inquiry (also called guided inquiry) in which they develop abilities and understanding of selected aspects of the inquiry process. The standards also say that students should be provided with opportunities to engage in full inquiry (also called open-ended inquiry) in which students choose a question, design an investigation, gather evidence, formulate an answer to the original question, and communicate the investigative process and results.

Encouraging students to conduct open-ended inquiry is uncommon in most classrooms. When students are given the opportunity, they are typically thrown into the situation with little more than a worksheet describing, "The Scientific Method" and perhaps some practice in setting up controlled experiments. This is not enough. Students need to know that there are more ways to investigate than just controlled experiments. They need practice in choosing and refining investigable questions, selecting an appropriate pathway to answer their question, in identifying possible variables, and quantifying outcome variables. They need practice in putting all the aspects of inquiry together. Without this guidance and practice, students often choose questions that can't be answered experimentally. They likewise may choose inappropriate ways to answer questions, have no way to quantify their evidence, and draw conclusions unrelated to the evidence. The result is often frustrating to students and teachers alike. Most often, students' abilities to inquire don't enable them to be more systematic or productive—and to move beyond exploration (which, as we've said, they already do quite well without instruction). And there are some who believe that forcing students through a rigid and linear process even impairs their natural born ability to inquire!

What Kind of Mixture Is Oobleck?

Oobleck is a suspension of cornstarch in water. A suspension is a type of mixture, as are solutions, colloids, and precipitates. In a mixture, two or more substances are combined. In a solution, a solid dissolves into a liquid. The atoms, molecules or ions become evenly dispersed in the liquid. In a suspension the ingredients keep their own properties and usually can be separated fairly easily.

Colloids and suspensions are both types of mixtures in which a solid is mixed into a liquid without dissolving. What distinguishes the two is that the particles in a colloid are smaller than those in a suspension. In a colloid the particles also tend to remain suspended (like milk), whereas those in a suspension tend to settle out. When Oobleck is kept moist and allowed to sit for a long time, the cornstarch will begin to separate from the water on its own. In a precipitate a solid forms in a solution due to a chemical reaction. This solid does not dissolve in the particular liquid.

A **mixture** is a combination of two or more substances. Solutions, colloids, suspensions, and precipitates are types of mixtures. In a **solution,** the atoms, molecules, or ions of a substance are evenly dispersed in a liquid, or **dissolved.** In a **colloid,** very tiny particles of a substance are dispersed in another substance—but not dissolved. The particles in a colloid are smaller than those in a suspension. Milk is a colloid of tiny solids in a liquid. Smoke is a colloid of tiny solids in a gas. Mist is a colloid of tiny particles of liquid in a gas. In a **suspension,** tiny particles, larger than those in a colloid are dispersed in another substance, but not dissolved. These particles can usually be separated from the liquid fairly easily. Oobleck is a suspension of cornstarch in water. Sand mixed in water is also a suspension. In a **precipitate** a solid forms in a solution due to a chemical reaction. This solid does not dissolve in the particular liquid.

The distinction between Newtonian and non-Newtonian fluids is less important than the opportunity for students to improve their scientific thinking abilities and understandings through their own investigations of this strange substance. More advanced students may find it of interest, or discover the distinction during independent web research. A full examination of a range of theories scientists have offered for the internal workings of non-Newtonian fluids would require a deeper understanding of chemistry and physics, and even then there is no single agreed-upon explanation!

In earlier editions, we over-emphasized the factor of temperature in this context. The crucial distinguishing factor is shear force, which changes the viscosity of non-Newtonian fluids, but not Newtonian ones. It is of course the case that both temperature and pressure affect the viscosity of liquids, and that in everyday life we notice how many fluids thicken when cooled and become less viscous when heated, but the non-Newtonian distinction relates only to shear force.

For an excellent, accessible discussion of non-Newtonian fluids, see the "outrageous Ooze" activity of the Exploratorium, on the Internet at: http://www.exploratorium.edu/science_explorer/ooze.html

What Are Non-Newtonian Fluids?

One of the most fascinating things about Oobleck is precisely the ambiguity that students explore when they consider whether Oobleck is a liquid or a solid. Substances that flow, such as liquids and gases, are called fluids. Oobleck is a fluid, but a fluid of an uncommon sort. Its usul nature relates to its viscosity and how its viscosity changes. Viscosity is a measure of how strongly layers of fluid resist flowing past each other when under stress, or shear forces. Words such as "thickness" or "gooiness" are often synonyms for viscosity.

Newtonian fluids, such as water, gasoline, and mineral oil, are those whose viscosity does not change as a result of a shear force exerted upon it. When you agitate a liquid by hitting it or moving your fingers through it, you are applying a shear force. Isaac Newton observed that for many fluids the flow increases in a regular way when the shear forces increase, indicating that the viscosity is a constant even when shear forces or fluid velocities change. In other words, no matter how hard you hit water or how quickly you move your fingers through it, it will have the same viscosity. Fluids that behave this way are called Newtonian fluids, and they include all gases and many liquids. Fluids that don't behave this way are called non–Newtonian fluids.

There are some non–Newtonian fluids that actually become *less* viscous when subject to shear forces. If you hit a deep pool of one of these fluids or quickly move your fingers through it, it will become less viscous. Although these are more unusual than Newtonian fluids there are some common examples, such as blood, shampoo, fruit juice concentrates, mayonnaise, gelatin, liquid cement, paint and ketchup. Common practical experience with this phenomena is when people shake a container to get one of these non-Newtonian fluids to flow more easily.

Even rarer are another type of non–Newtonian fluids, like Oobleck, that become *more* viscous when subject to shear forces. Your students discovered this as they noticed more resistance when they increased the shear force by hitting it hard or moving their fingers through it quickly. These fluids make transitions from liquid to a solid-like state that defy expectations of how a substance ought to behave. Quicksand also becomes more viscous with agitation, which is why trying to move quickly if stuck in quicksand would make it more difficult to move. To confuse matters more, most of these fluids will also become *less* viscous if only a low shear rate is applied

There are also non-Newtonian fluids known as plastic fluids. These are fluids that won't flow until a certain shear stress is applied. Some examples are toothpaste, hand cream, grease, and some ketchups. Toothpaste will not flow without pressure, but once the right amount of pressure is applied, it flows easily.

Time dependent non-Newtonian fluids either become less viscous with time (like yogurt or paint in a sealed container), or more viscous with time (like gypsum paste).

What Makes Oobleck Behave As It Does?

Why Oobleck has such properties remains somewhat of a mystery. Some scientists have approached this question on a particle level and some at a molecular level. Here are three of their explanations:

1. Sand in Water Model
In this model, the starch particles in Oobleck are compared to sand and water in a plastic squeeze bottle. The grains of sand are packed closely together, with a little water in between. The surface tension of the water does not allow all of the spaces between the grains to be filled. Squeezing the bottle gently forces the grains of sand to slide against each other, increasing the spacing between some of the grains, and allowing more water to fill the spaces. The more gently you squeeze, the more time there is for the water to fill the spaces between the grains and provide lubrication so they will slide against each other, and flow. But when the bottle is squeezed quickly, there is not enough water between the spaces to start with, and friction between the grains of sand resists the flow.

Although the grains of starch in Oobleck are much smaller than grains of sand, starch molecules are relatively large, as molecules go. Therefore, a mixture of water and cornstarch may act very much like a mixture of sand and water. This is one explanation for why Oobleck flows like a fluid, yet when suddenly compressed offers the resistance we associate with a solid.

For a brief and excellent discussion of shear force and an experiment in space designed to learn more about the properties of liquids, see this NASA website, entitled "Shear Mystery: at: http://science.nasa. gov/headlines/y2002/07jun_ elastic_fluids.htm?friend

For a discussion of different kinds of non-Newtonian fluids, with viscosity graphs, and more on this general scientific topic of flow in matter, or rheology, see: http:// www.sju.edu/~phabdas/physics/ rheo.html

The sand-and-water process described here is directly comparable to the liquefaction of sediment that can take place during earthquakes. See, for example, www.tulane.edu/~sanelson/ images/liquefaction.gif

Two articles in The Physics Teacher *report some interesting findings about how a bowl of dried beans can act as a liquid and related issues. See "On the Difference Between Fluids and Dried Beans" by Rolf Winter (February 1990) and "Liquid beans" by Robert Prigo (volume 26, 1988). There is considerable scientific literature and fascinating findings on sand (see for example, a New York Times article of September 7, 1996—"From Grains of Sand: A World of Order").*

2. Long Chains Model

This model bases the behavior of Oobleck on chemical structure. Cornstarch is made of long chains called polymers. This model speculates that when a mixture of cornstarch and water is compressed, the chains are stretched in a direction that is at right angles to the direction of compression. The molecules become "tangled," are unable to slide easily against each other, and offer the resistance we associate with a solid.

3. Electrical Charge Model

This model suggests that the particles in Oobleck acquire an electrical charge as they rub together. The faster they are rubbed, the more electrical attraction is created between the particles, causing an increase in the viscosity of the mixture.

These are among the ways scientists have attempted to explain the unusual properties of Oobleck and similar substances. An excellent discussion is provided by Jearl Walker in two articles in "The Amateur Scientist" section of *Scientific American* and there is quite a bit of scientific literature on related subjects, including an article by Albert Einstein. If you're interested in reading more on this subject, here are a few references.

Billmeyer, Fred W. *Textbook of Polymer Science,* 3rd edition, John Wiley and Sons, New York, 1984.

Einstein, A. (1905) "On the Motion of Small Particles Suspended in Liquids at Rest Required by the Molecular-Kinetic Theory of Heat." *Annalen der Physik 17*, 549-560. Einstein, A. (1905) "A New Determination of Molecular Dimensions." *Annalen der Physik 17*, 549-560. These papers, published two weeks apart, are often considered as one because their subjects are related. Both are extensions of Einstein's doctoral dissertation. They are among the papers he published in 1905—afterwards called the "miracle year" given what he accomplished—at the age of 26. Together the papers introduced many of his most famous ideas, including relativity and $e = mc^2$. In his work on molecular dimensions and small particles, Einstein sought to explain Brownian motion, the zigzag motion of microscopic particles in suspension, as in a colloid. He suggested it was caused by the random motion of molecules of the suspension medium as they bounced against the suspended particles. Using a statistical method, he showed he could estimate the number and size of molecules in a cubic centimeter of liquid. This made an important contribution to proving that molecules *actually do exist,* which was not generally accepted at the time. For more on this see the Gary Moring reference on the next page.

There are many places on the web, especially food-related sites, where the chemical structure of starch is explained. Here are two of the most helpful: http://www.jic.ac.uk/STAFF/cliff-hedley/Starch.html and http://www.cem.msu.edu/~reusch/VirtualText/carbhyd.htm

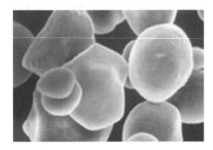

Most animals, including humans, depend on plant starches for food. Starch is a polymer of glucose, found in roots, rhizomes, seeds, stems, tubers, and corms of plants, as microscopic granules with characteristic shapes and sizes. The structure usually consists of two materials—amylose and amylopectin. Amylose, whose molecules are linear chains, makes up about 25%. Amylopectin, which makes up about 75%, is a much higher molecular weight substance, whose molecules are branched networks.

Katz, David A. *Chemistry in the Toy Store,* 2nd edition, 1983. Available from Department of Chemistry, Community College of Philadelphia, 1700 Spring Garden Street, Philadelphia, PA 19107.

Kerr, Paul F. *Quick Clay, Scientific American,* volume 209, number 5, pages 132-142, November, 1963.

Moring, Gary F. *The Complete Idiot's Guide to Understanding Einstein,* Indianapolis, Alpha Books, Macmillan USA, 2000, pages 140–161.)

Walker, Jearl. The Amateur Scientist, *Scientific American,* volume 239, number 5, pages 186-198, November, 1978, and volume 246, number 1, pages 174-180, January 1982.

Model of Starch Molecule

States of Matter

Matter is all substances that take up space and have mass. Solids, liquids and gases are terms used to group matter according to definite mass, volume, and shape. They are states (or phases) of matter. **Solids** have definite mass, volume and shape. The particles in a solid vibrate, but do not move too much. They are packed closely together often in regular patterns. **Liquids** have definite mass and volume, but not shape. The particles in a liquid slide past each other and vibrate. They are packed closely but without regular patterns. **Gases** have definite mass, but not volume or shape. The particles in a gas vibrate and move very quickly, are well separated and are not in regular patterns. Substances can change between these states. This normally is caused by the increase or decrease of the energy of the particles brought on by heating or cooling. These changes in state are physical changes, as opposed to chemical changes. There are other states of matter, including: plasma—which exists throughout the Universe in stars and on Earth under some conditions, such as fluorescent bulbs and lightning, and Bose-Einstein condensate—which only forms at temperatures near absolute zero.

From http://www.ccmr.cornell.edu/ education/ask/index.html?quid=14 The molecules that make up cornstarch are very different from the small water molecules. They consist of long chains of repeating units called sugars. Sucrose or table sugar has two such repeating units per molecule, whereas starch has many, many more. In pure cornstarch, the sugar chains stick strongly and cannot move past one another, thus starch is a solid. However, if we add water to starch, the water gets between the starch chains, separates them and allows the chains to slide past one another; the mixture behaves as a liquid. If we apply pressure to the starch mixture, the water is squeezed out from between the chains and they are able to grab one another. Sliding is prevented and the material behaves as a solid. If we release the pressure, the water can enter between the chains to allow sliding once more. This behavior is not limited to the molecular scale. A similar phenomena occurs when you run on wet sand at the beach. If you run fast and generate pressure quickly the sand feels hard as water is squeezed out and the sand particles cling to each other. If you step slowly to apply the pressure gradually, the sand particles have time to move past one another— your foot sinks!

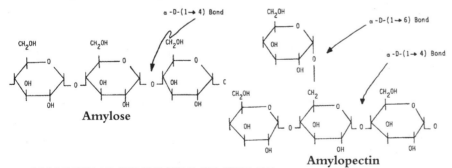

MOLECULAR STRUCTURE OF STARCH
Amylose is a linear polymer of short 1,4 linked glucose chains. The amylose fraction is usually about 25–30% of the starch molecules found in corn and has a molecular weight of about 250,000. Amylopectin is about 70–75% of the starch found in the corn kernel and has a molecular weight of about 50–500 million. It is a branched polymer of the basic repeating units of 1,4 linked glucose with branches of 1,6 linked glucose. The branching occurs irregularly, about one per 25 glucose units.

Scientific Facts, Laws, and Theories

These three terms describe important aspects of the nature of science, but are often misunderstood. Each has a meaning in common usage that is different from its meaning in the scientific community, and this can cause confusion. These are the definitions as written by the National Academy of Sciences.

Fact: In science, an observation that has been repeatedly confirmed and for all practical purposes is accepted as "true." Truth in science, however, is never final, and what is accepted as a fact today may be modified or even discarded tomorrow.

Law: A descriptive generalization about how some aspect of the natural world behaves under stated circumstances.

Theory: In science, a well-substantiated explanation of some aspect of the natural world that can incorporate facts, laws, inferences, and tested hypotheses.

The contention that evolution should be taught as a "theory, not as a fact" confuses the common use of these words with the scientific use. In science, theories do not turn into facts through the accumulation of evidence. Rather, theories are the end points of science. They are understandings that develop from extensive observation, experimentation, evidence and creative reflection. They incorporate a large body of scientific facts, laws, tested hypotheses, and logical inferences. In this sense, evolution is one of the strongest and most useful scientific theories we have.

★Adapted from Teaching About Evolution and the Nature of Science *by the National Academy of Sciences (Washington, D.C.: National Academy Press, 1998).*

For more information, there's an excellent website on states of matter at: http://www.chem.purdue.edu/gchelp/atoms/states.html

The History of Mars Exploration

Mars—the red planet—has fascinated humans throughout the ages. For hundreds of years, observations were limited by the vast distance separating Earth from Mars. About once every two years, at its closest regular approach (called opposition), Mars passes within about 55 million kilometers of Earth and that is when Earth-based telescopes have been able to capture the best photographs. More recently, the Hubble Space Telescope has provided excellent views from its orbit around Earth.

Mars has been the object of many theories and questions. Claims that the "canals" on Mars were built by intelligent beings aroused controversy early in the 20th century. Did life exist on Mars in the past or present? Was there water on Mars—if so, in what form? What was the Martian atmosphere composed of? Could Mars tell us more about the evolution of Earth and the Solar System? Mars not only fascinated scientists from many disciplines, but also the general public. There was a huge reaction to "War of the Worlds," the radio broadcast by Orson Welles of the H. G. Wells book that dramatized a fictitious invasion from Mars. Earth-based observations of Mars paved the way for spacecraft exploration of the planet. Fueled by the curiosities of both the scientific community and the public, on November 28, 1964 Mariner 4 was launched and 228 days later it became the first spacecraft to visit the red planet.

The Mariner Mars Missions

Mariner 4 was able to obtain and transmit close range images of Mars. After its launch and a journey of hundreds of millions of kilometers, Mariner 4 passed within 9,844 kilometers of Mars on July 14, 1965. It took four days to transmit the image information to Earth and the spacecraft returned useful data until December 20, 1967. Mariner 6 and Mariner 7 were identical spacecraft launched on February 24, 1969 and March 27, 1969 and their missions were the flyby study of Mars. The probes passed closest to Mars on July 30 and August 4 of the same year.

Mariner 9 was to have an identical companion, Mariner 8, but on May 8, 1971, 365 seconds after launch, Mariner 8 fell into the Atlantic. Mariner 9 was the first of NASA's Mars orbiters. The spacecraft was launched on May 30, 1971 and arrived in Mars orbit on November 14, 1971. After 349 days in Mars orbit, 7,329 images (including images of Mars' two moons, Phobos and Deimos) had been relayed back to Earth. The images, covering about 80% of the planet, revealed ancient river beds, craters, massive extinct volcanoes, canyons, layered polar deposits, evidence of wind-driven deposition and erosion of sediments, weather fronts, dust storms, and more. With evidence of flow features, and therefore the possibility of a time when water was in liquid form on the surface of Mars, the question of the existence of life intensified. Many new questions had been raised that a lander would be better suited to answer. The new information from Mariner 9 served as the foundation for the Viking program.

Viking Mission to Mars

NASA's Viking Mission to Mars involved two spacecraft, Viking 1 and Viking 2, each with an orbiter and a lander. The primary objectives were to obtain high resolution images of the Martian surface, characterize the structure and composition of the atmosphere and surface, and search for evidence of life. Viking 1 was launched on August 20, 1975 and arrived at Mars on June 19, 1976. On July 20, 1976 the Viking 1 Lander separated from the Orbiter and touched down. Viking 2 was launched September 9, 1975 and entered Mars orbit on August 7, 1976. The Viking 2 Lander touched down on September 3, 1976. The Orbiters imaged the entire surface of Mars. The Viking Landers transmitted images of the surface, took surface samples and analyzed them for composition and signs of life, studied atmospheric composition and meteorology, and used seismometers. The Viking 2 Lander ended communications on April 11, 1980, and the Viking 1 Lander on November 13, 1982, after transmitting over 1,400 images of the two sites. Many of the Viking Orbiter and Lander images are available from the National Space Science Data Center (NSSDC), online or on CD-ROM, and as photographs (http://nssdc.gsfc.nasa.gov/). Seasonal dust storms, pressure changes, and transport of atmospheric gases between the polar caps were observed. A biology experiment produced no evidence of life at either landing site.

Previous editions of this GEMS guide included a poster of the Viking mission and students compared their work to that of Viking mission scientists. With the landing and extensive work of the two Mars Rovers, we've updated that class session, but if you have the poster you could use it as well.

Mars Pathfinder Mission

The Mars Pathfinder mission consisted of a stationary lander and a surface rover. Its goal was to demonstrate the feasibility of relatively low-cost landings on and exploration of the Martian surface. This goal was achieved by tests of communications between the rover and lander, and the lander and Earth, tests of the imaging devices and sensors, and tests of the maneuverability and systems of the rover on the surface. Mars Pathfinder was launched on December 4, 1996. The spacecraft entered the Martian atmosphere on July 4, 1997 without going into orbit. The cruise stage was jettisoned 30 minutes before atmospheric entry. The lander took atmospheric measurements as it descended. The entry vehicle's heat shield slowed the craft. An 11 meter (36 feet) diameter parachute was deployed, slowing the craft further. The heat shield was released after parachute deployment, and the bridle, a 20 meter long braided Kevlar tether, deployed below the spacecraft. The lander separated from the backshell and slid down to the bottom of the bridle. About 10 seconds before landing four air bags inflated forming a protective "ball" around the lander. The three solid rockets, mounted in the backshell fired to slow the descent, and the bridle was cut 21.5 m above the ground, releasing the airbag-encased lander. The lander dropped to the ground and struck on July 4, 1997 and bounced about 12 meters (40 feet) into the air, bouncing at least another 15 times and rolling before coming to rest about 2.5 minutes after impact and about 1 km from the initial impact site. The Mars Pathfinder returned more than 16,000 images from the lander and 550 images from the small rover, named Sojourner, as well as more than 15 chemical analyses of rocks and extensive data on winds and other weather factors.

Mars Global Surveyor

The Mars Global Surveyor (MGS) mission entered orbit and began its mapping mission in 1999, with data acquired until April 2002. The spacecraft will also be used as a data relay for later U.S. and international missions. Mars Global Surveyor is the first spacecraft in a series of missions to be launched in a planned decade-long exploration of Mars by NASA. Launches will be orbiters, landers, rovers, and probes to Mars.

The Mars Exploration Rovers

NASA's twin robot "geologists," the Mars Exploration Rovers, launched toward Mars on June 10 and July 7, 2003, and landed on Mars January 3 and January 24, 2004 PST (January 4 and January 25 UTC). The primary scientific goal was to search for and characterize a wide range of rocks and soils that hold clues to past water activity. The spacecraft were targeted to sites on opposite sides of Mars that appear to have been affected by liquid water in the past. The landing sites were at Gusev Crater, a possible former lake in a giant crater, and Meridiani Planum, where mineral deposits (hematite) suggest a wet past.

After the airbag-protected landing craft settled onto the surface and opened, the rovers rolled out to take panoramic images. These gave information to select promising geological targets that will tell part of the story of water in Mars' past. Then, the Rovers were guided to those locations to perform on-site scientific investigations. Their mission was planned for 90 days, but the rovers continued to operate and provide information into 2008, when this guide was revised.

Scientific instruments carried by the rovers include: a panoramic camera for determining the mineralogy, texture, and structure of the local terrain; a miniature thermal emission spectrometer for identifying promising rocks and soils for closer examination and to provide temperature profiles of the Martian atmosphere; magnets for collecting magnetic dust particles; a microscopic imager (MI): for obtaining close-up, high-resolution images of rocks and soils; a rock abrasion tool for removing dusty and weathered rock surfaces and exposing fresh material; and a number of other instruments.

Each rover is sort of the mechanical equivalent of a geologist walking the surface of Mars. The mast-mounted cameras are 1.5 meters (5 feet) high and provide 360-degree, stereoscopic, humanlike views of the terrain. The robotic arm can move in much the same way as a human arm with an elbow and wrist, and places instruments directly up against rock and soil targets of interest. In the mechanical "fist" of the arm is a microscopic camera that serves the same purpose as a geologist's handheld magnifying lens. The Rock Abrasion Tool serves as the geologist's rock hammer to expose the insides of rocks.

Before landing, the goal for each rover was to drive up to 40 meters (about 44 yards) in a single day, for a total of up to one 1 kilometer (about three-quarters of a mile). Both goals have been far exceeded! For much more on the Mars Rovers, encourage your students to visit: http://marsrovers.jpl.nasa.gov/home/

Future Mars missions are planned, including long-term planning for missions with astronauts aboard. There have been many other missions to Mars in the past, in addition to those summarized here. Some have been successful; some have failed; some have been partly successful. In addition to the United States, Mars missions have also involved the (former) Soviet Union, Japan, and Europe. For a list of all Mars missions, see: http://mars.jpl.nasa.gov/missions/log/

Teacher's Outline

Activity 1: Lab Investigation

■ Getting Ready

1. Mix Oobleck well before class.
2. Mix 4 boxes cornstarch, 6 $\frac{1}{2}$ cups water, 15 drops food coloring. Let stand. Stir with hand 15 minutes before class.
3. Cover work areas with newspaper.
4. Establish optional equipment station.

■ Setting the Scene

1. A space probe has just returned from a newly discovered moon in the Solar System. We'll investigate a sample from the moon's green ocean.
2. We've named the substance "Oobleck."
3. Preliminary studies show Oobleck is safe to handle. Students will find out what it is made from later.
4. Explain the meaning of "properties" by using paper as example.
5. Tell students their job is to identify properties of Oobleck. Use all senses **except taste.**
6. Organize research lab teams. Tell students to record properties on large sheets of paper and number them.
7. Give each team one container of Oobleck. Encourage exploration.
8. After five minutes hand out large sheets of paper and markers. Help teams as needed.
9. Ask lab teams to star properties that are important in determining if Oobleck is solid or liquid.
10. Cleanup.

Activity 2: Scientific Convention

■ Getting Ready

1. Post lists of properties on wall or board.
2. Keep Oobleck and newspaper on hand in case needed for further testing .

■ Setting the Scene

1. Professional scientists hold conventions. The goal is to find the truth and state it clearly and completely.
2. Tell students their convention on Oobleck will follow these rules:
    a. One property discussed at a time.
    b. Raise hands to say why you agree or disagree with a property.
    c. Try to re-phrase properties so everyone agrees.
    d. Vote on whether or not class agrees with a property to see if it's a "Law of Oobleck." (Some teachers may prefer other terms.)

■ Facilitating the Discussion

- Time for discussion will depend on interest level.
- Allow students to resolve disagreements by going back to the lab for a few minutes.
- Challenge students to think of cases where a stated property might not be true.
- Change wording so everyone can agree by adding a phrase or defining terms.
- Allow for further experimentation to resolve disagreements.

Ask questions and probe for student reasoning.

Activity 3: Spacecraft Design

■ Getting Ready

Write Laws of Oobleck (from previous activity) on board.

■ Setting the Scene

1. Challenge is to design a spacecraft capable of safely landing on an ocean of Oobleck, explore the moon, and take off again, with all passengers safely on board.
2. Review Laws of Oobleck. Emphasize that spaceship designs must take these into account.
3. Tell students to draw ideas and label parts that allow craft to land safely and take off again without getting stuck.
4. Hand out paper and colors. Students can work in teams or individually.

■ Designing and Discussing Spacecraft

1. Help as needed. Remind students to label drawings.
2. Allow students to continue for a second session if needed.
3. Encourage students to see each other's drawings.
4. Ask volunteers to explain spacecraft ideas. Give everyone who wants to a chance.
5. Ask which designs are most likely to survive.

Activity 4: What Scientists Do

■ Getting Ready

1. Write these headings across top of board: "Laboratory," "Convention," and "Spacecraft Design"

2. Prepare overhead transparencies of the Mars Rover mission.

3. Choose quotation(s) on nature of science and make overhead of it.

■ Setting the Scene

1. Reveal that Oobleck is made of cornstarch, water, and green food coloring.

2. Remind students that the Oobleck activity had three parts: laboratory, convention, and spacecraft design.

■ Students as Scientists

1. Ask students to describe how they acted as scientists in the laboratory. List their ideas on the board.

2. Do the same for the Convention and Spacecraft Design parts of the activity.

3. Explain that these scientific methods are used by professional scientists too. Briefly discuss their ideas about designing a craft to land on Mars.

4. Point out how Mars mission scientists used these processes. Refer to the overhead images and step-by-step text provided for them.

5. Conclude by discussing the nature of science as an ever-changing process of knowledge based on evidence derived from observation and experiment to seek to explain the natural world. Post the quotation by Albert Einstein and/or others of your choice.

Consider presenting optional activities:

Activity 5: Microscope Eyes

Activity 6: Full Investigations

Anticipated Student Outcomes

1. Students improve their ability to observe, hypothesize, and experiment with a new substance to determine its properties.

2. Students are able to critically discuss, analyze, and modify their initial list of properties in light of comments and questions from other students.

3. Students recognize that substances cannot simply be classified as a solid or liquid, and that a given substance may exhibit solid or liquid properties under different conditions.

4. Students apply their understanding of a substance's properties to design a spacecraft that will land on an ocean of Oobleck.

5. Students learn about the fields of science and engineering and become aware of the many processes and skills used by scientists and engineers.

Additional outcomes for optional sessions:

— Students improve their ability to design models that can provide an explanation for the solid/liquid properties of Oobleck.

— Students are able to design and conduct a full investigation.

Embedded Assessment Activities

Lists of Properties: In Activity 1, student teams investigate Oobleck and list its properties. This provides information about whether or not students understand the concept of a property, and the degree to which they have analyzed their list to assure its accuracy. (Outcome 1)

Scientific Convention: In Activity 2, students critically discuss and compare the properties of their substances. During the discussion, the teacher can notice whether students move beyond their initial statements to listen to each other, consider various points of view, and try to reach consensus about the most accurate statement. (Outcomes 2, 5)

Is Oobleck a Liquid or Solid?: During the convention, teachers can look for statements that describe the liquid or solid properties of Oobleck. They can observe whether students can articulate the conditions under which Oobleck acts as a solid or as a liquid. (Outcome 3)

Designing a Spacecraft: During Activity 3, teachers can observe whether students apply the information they know about the properties of Oobleck as they design a spacecraft to land on an ocean of Oobleck. (Outcome 4)

Microscope Eyes: During the optional Activity 5, students design their own models to explain what may be happening on a microscopic level to cause Oobleck's strange properties. This provides information about student understanding about the conditions under which Oobleck acts as a solid or as a liquid, as well as molecular models. It also provides an opportunity to see how well the students are able to craft an explanation that matches the available evidence.

Full Investigations: During the optional Activity 6, student teams design their own full investigation into a question about Oobleck. Through their preliminary notes and especially through their poster presentations, students demonstrate their understanding of the nature and processes of scientific inquiry and investigation, as well their understanding of the science content under investigation.

Additional Assessment Ideas

What Do Scientists and Engineers Do? Have students pretend they are applying for a job in a science or engineering firm. Have them write a detailed letter to the personnel director and explain how they gained experience as scientists and engineers when they investigated Oobleck. The letters will help show students' level of awareness of the some main processes of science, such as experimenting, observing, and inferring. (Outcome 5)

Properties of Sand: Substitute sand in the activities in the guide. Ask students if sand is a liquid or solid. Have them justify their point of view. (Outcomes 1, 2, 3, 4, 5)

See "The Sand Task" (from *Insights and Outcomes*, the GEMS Assessment Handbook) on the following pages.

The Sand Task from *Oobleck:* *What Do Scientists Do?*

*S*tudents explore the properties of an unusual substance that has the properties of both a solid and a liquid in the *Oobleck* GEMS guide. In the first session, students form small laboratory teams to learn how scientists describe the properties of a substance. They observe, hypothesize, and experiment with Oobleck to determine its unique qualities. During the second session, the lab teams hold a scientific convention to discuss and analyze their findings. Students challenge each other to define the properties of Oobleck more accurately and refine their communication skills.

To assess students' ability to apply their knowledge of properties in a new situation, we presented fifth graders with a sand exploration. To prepare for the task, the teacher provides pairs of students with:

- a small cup of sand

- an empty cup

- a stick for use as a probe

- a magnifying lens

In addition, each student receives a record sheet, as shown on the next page.

Students are told they are to act like scientists whose job is to explore the sand. They may use any of the tools provided or other materials that they might find in the classroom in their explorations. Pairs of students investigate the sand and make a list of its properties. Each student makes an individual list on his or her record sheet (Part I: Investigating Sand) while the pair works together to explore the sand.

As in the *Oobleck* unit, the teacher then leads a class discussion where each team presents its ideas. The entire class discusses in detail one or more of the properties of sand that addresses whether or not sand should be considered a liquid, a solid, or both.

The students then work individually to answer Part II: Sand Questions on their record sheets.

My Name _____

My Partner's Name _____

Part I: Investigating Sand

1. Work with your partner and use the materials at your table to explore the sand. Use your senses and what you discover as you explore to make a list of the Properties of Sand.

Part II: Sand Questions
Answer these questions.
Use information you discovered when you explored the sand.

1. In what ways is sand like a liquid?

2. In what ways is sand like a solid?

What do I want to see?

This two-part assessment task provides students with an opportunity to apply skills learned through the *Oobleck* unit and demonstrate their ability to:
— Observe the properties of a substance.
— Record and communicate observations.
— Determine conditions under which sand behaves like a liquid or a solid.
— Describe how a substance can have properties of both liquids and solids.

How do I evaluate the student work?

Teachers may decide to group student work into three categories.

COMPLETE RESPONSES to this task would include the following qualities.
Part I: The record sheet includes a wide variety of both sensory and experiential observations (what they observed as they conducted simple manipulations with the sand). Language explicitly describes the students' findings.

Part II: The students are able to respond extensively to the questions with detailed examples of what they did and observed with samples of sand. They present a strong, clear case to explain why sand has properties similar to both liquids and solids, under different conditions.

PARTIAL RESPONSES would include the following qualities.
Part I: The record sheet includes a limited list of sensory and/or experiential observations. The list may omit one or more essential qualities of sand (i.e., its color, its ability to pour). Students adequately summarize their findings but descriptions are limited to the more observable features of sand.

Part II: The students respond to the questions with limited insight and a few examples of what they did and observed with samples of sand. They maintain that sand has properties of both liquids and solids but provide only partial or unclear justification for their conclusion.

MINIMAL RESPONSES would include the following qualities.
Part I: The record sheet includes a short list of sensory OR experiential observations. The list may omit one or more essential qualities of sand (e.g., its color, its ability to pour). The descriptions provide little detail about the properties.

Part II: The students respond to the questions with minimal insight and few or no examples of what they did and observed with samples of sand. They may describe sand as similar to a liquid or a solid, but do not discuss the fact that sand could have both liquid AND solid properties. Or, they may agree that sand is like a liquid and a solid but do not support their conclusion with clear scientific evidence.

What insights have I gained?

This assessment can be used to guide instructional decisions about how to structure scientific explorations or future implementation plans for the *Oobleck* unit.

If appropriate, this assessment can be evaluated for use with a traditional grading system. Teachers can evaluate the responses and assign point values to each section of the assessment.

COMPLETE = 3 points

PARTIAL = 2 points

MARGINAL = 1 point

NO RESPONSE = 0 points

Thus, the total number of possible points for this assessment would be six (three for each section). Performance levels could be established with a range of "6" (exemplary) to "0" (no response) and assigned a percentage or letter grade value.

For example, some students may score well on one section but need improvement on another section. This student might develop a comprehensive list of the properties of sand, and score a "3" on Part I of the assessment. However, their analysis in Part II may need additional justification and thus would score a "2." The total for this student would be a "5" of a possible six points which could translate to an 83% score.

Although this method of assessment can be used as the basis of a traditional grade, it is far richer in the feedback it provides for the teacher and student. The activity shows how the students apply their abilities to explore new substances in a real-life situation. It shows how they use their senses, apply concepts and reflect on their discoveries to support their conclusions. The students will gain more information about their progress from a detailed analysis of what they did well than from a letter grade alone. For all students, the concepts and skills involved in the Sand Task assessment go far beyond letter grades, the narrow definition of what a "property" is, or physical science understandings of matter. As with Oobleck, this seemingly simple observation and analysis of a substance (in this case, sand), exemplifies the essence of the nature of science, or "what scientists do." As students plan, conduct, record, and discuss their explorations, they gain a direct, tactile, yet also quite sophisticated and practical understanding of how a scientist approaches the real world. Because student abilities and conceptual understandings grow and develop over time, explorations such as the Sand Task can be evaluated on many levels and presented at different grade levels.

RESOURCES AND LITERATURE CONNECTIONS

More About Inquiry

National Resource Council (1996) *The National Science Education Standards*, Washington D.C., National Academy Press.

National Resource Council (2000) *Inquiry and the National Science Education Standards: A Guide for Teaching and Learning*, Steve Olson and Susan Loucks-Horsley (eds), Washington D.C., National Academy Press.

Exploratorium Institute for Inquiry at: http://www.exploratorium.edu/IFI/resources/websites.html

Inquire Within: Implementing Inquiry-Based Science Standards by Douglas Llewellyn (Author) Corwin Press (July 2001)

Nurturing Inquiry: Real Science for the Elementary Classroom by Charles R. Pearce (Author) Heinemann; (April 1999)

Science As Inquiry: Active Learning, Project-Based, Web-Assisted, and Active Assessment Strategies to Enhance Student Learning by Jack Hassard, Goodyear Publishing (October 1999)

Weaving Science Inquiry and Continuous Assessment: Using Formative Assessment to Improve Learning by Maura O'Brien Carlson, Gregg E. Humphrey, Karen S. Reinhardt, Corwin Press; (May 2003)

Bonnstetter, Ronald J.: "Inquiry: Learning from the Past with an Eye on the Future" EJSE (*Electronic Journal of Science Education*); volume 3 number 1, September, 1998.

More About Mars

Videos, CDs, and DVDs on Mars

A range of multimedia resources on Mars and the history of exploration of the planet are available from:

The MMI Space Science Corporation
Phone 410-366-1222
Fax 410-366-6311
2950 Wyman Parkway
Baltimore, MD 21211

Mars—Past, Present, and Future—CR190 or DVD8
Available in both VCR and DVD format, this 83-minute video traces the history of human fascination with Mars, from the earliest telescope sightings to the past, present, and future missions to Mars. The DVD includes the NASA film Planet Mars as a bonus.

Mars—Past, Present, and Future—CDR170
An interactive CD-ROM, for PC or Mac, includes a wealth of images along with narration, video, and sound effects.

Pathfinder and the Best of Mars—CDR-168
This CD-ROM includes 150 images of Mars plus 20 3-D pictures with viewing glasses included. Includes images from the Viking, Pathfinder, and Mariner missions, as well as images from the Hubble telescope.

Mars related slides, videos, and CD-ROMs are also available through:
Astronomical Society of the Pacific
390 Ashton Avenue
San Francisco, CA 94112
Phone 415-337-1100
fax 415-337-5205
http://www.astrosociety.org/index.html

NASA Mars Websites

NASA's Mars Exploration program maintains a rich website at **http://mars.jpl.nasa.gov/** which includes areas for "Kids," "Students," and "Educators," and offers images, videos, facts, online activities and games, curriculum units, educator workshops, and lots more.

Other interesting NASA-related Mars websites include:

http://www.nasa.gov/mro

http://nssdc.gsfc.nasa.gov/planetary/mars/marshist.html

http://mars.jpl.nasa.gov/mep/history/

http://mars.jpl.nasa.gov/mep/history/1900.html

http://mars.jpl.nasa.gov/mep/missions/announce2.html

http://nssdc.gsfc.nasa.gov/planetary/planets/marspage.html

http://www.jpl.nasa.gov/pictures/solar/2003rover/

http://photojournal.jpl.nasa.gov/

Books on Mars

Continuing NASA exploration of Mars has led to an explosion of books on the planet, many with great photographs. Here are just a few:

Postcards from Mars: The First Photographer on the Red Planet by Jim Bell, Dutton, 2006. Outstanding photographs from the Mars Rovers.

Magnificent Mars by Ken Crosswell, Free Press, 2003. This splendid book that combines more than 200 pages of photos with current science.

Mars: Uncovering the Secrets of the Red Planet by Paul Raeburn, National Geographic, 1998

A Traveler's Guide to Mars by William K. Hartmann Workman Publishing, New York, 1993

The Pathfinder Mission to Mars (Mission to Mars) by John Hamilton, Abdo & Daughters, 1998

There are a number of books available from NASA on Mars, including:
On Mars: Exploration of the Red Planet, 1958-1978 NASA History Series, Scientific and Technical Information Branch, 1984.

This official history of the Viking Project provides a wealth of information on the background for and realization of the Viking Missions. The book is available for free in pdf format online at the NASA History Office website: http://www.hq.nasa.gov/office/pao/History/SP-4212/on-mars.html

More About the Science of Matter

The Complete Idiot's Guide to Understanding Einstein by Gary F. Moring
Alpha Books, Macmillan USA, Pearson Education, 2000

Accessible, humorous, and focused on big scientific ideas, older students may find this book enjoyable. There are several parts of the text that describe Einstein's early work on molecular motion that relates to colloidal suspensions.

Einstein for Beginners by Joseph Schwartz and Michael McGuinness
Pantheon Books, 1990

One of the first titles in this very popular series of documentary comic books, *Einstein for Beginners* offers a fun and accessible introduction to Einstein's life and theories, placing them in the context of the important scientific discoveries that preceded them and contemporary world events.

Matter by Christopher Cooper, (in the Eyewitness Science series), Dorling Kindersley, New York, 1992.
Grades 4-8

Examines the elements that make up the physical world and the properties and behavior of different kinds of matter.

Website:
http://www.colorado.edu/physics/2000/index.pl

More Matter Activity Books

Adventures with Atoms and Molecules: Chemistry Experiments for Young People
by Robert C. Mebane and Thomas R. Rybolt (in the Adventures with Science series) Enslow, Hillside, New Jersey, 1985.
Grades 6-8

Chemistry experiments for home or school demonstrate the properties and behavior of various kinds of atoms and molecules. Concepts covered include properties of molecules, how temperature affects the behavior of molecules, and how the molecules in different liquids act.

From Glasses to Gases: The Science of Matter
by David Darling, (in the Experiment! Series), Silver Burdett Press, New York, 1992.
Grades 4-8

Text and experiments introduce matter and the various forms it can take under different conditions.

Janice Van Cleave's Molecules
by Janice Van Cleave, (in the Spectacular Science Projects series), John Wiley & Sons, New York, 1993.
Grades 4-8

This collection of science experiments and projects explores the mysteries of molecules.

Lotions, Potions, and Slime: Mudpies and More
by Nancy Blakely
Tricycle Press, 1996

A compendium of simple activities for home, day care, or classroom fun that features various wet and gooey liquids.

Solids, Liquids, and Gases from the Ontario Science Center
by Louise Osborne and Carol Gold, Kids Can Press, Buffalo, New York, 1995.
Grades 2-4

Uses experiments to illustrate concepts such as air pressure, condensation, and changes from liquids to solids and gases.

GEMS Home Science Kits

In partnership with Scientific Explorer, GEMS has developed a line of home-science kits based on GEMS activities, including:

Oobleck: Ooey Gooey Chemistry Slime Science Kit
Adapted from the activities in the Oobleck guide, this home science kit makes fascinating Oobleck activities available for birthdays, science fairs, and family fun.

Literature Connections

Bartholomew and the Oobleck
by Dr. Seuss
Random House, New York. 1949
Grades: K—9

A king orders his royal magicians to cause something new to rain down from the sky. A green rain called "Oobleck" falls onto the kingdom, in too much abundance, and its strange properties cause quite a mess until the ruler learns some humility.

Horrible Harry and the Green Slime
by Suzy Kline
illustrated by Frank Remkiewicz
Viking Penguin, New York. 1989
Grades: 2—4

Four stories about Miss Mackle's second grade

class. In "Demonstrations," Horrible Harry and his assistant Song Lee show how to make green slime from cornstarch, water, and food coloring. It's a big success, ending with the librarian taking it home to her husband who is interested in science. In another story, they celebrate reading *Charlotte's Web* by making cobwebs and hanging them all over the school.

The Quicksand Book
by Tomie dePaola
Holiday House, New York. 1977
Grades: 2—5

A jungle girl learns about the composition of quicksand, how different animals escape it, and how humans can use precautions to avoid getting stuck.

Her "teacher," an overly confident jungle boy, turns out not to be so superior. A variety of graphics and a helpful monkey give visual interest. A recipe for making your own quicksand is included.

The Search For Delicious
by Natalie Babbitt
Farrar, Straus & Giroux, New York. 1969
Grades: 5—8

After an argument between the king and queen over the meaning of the world "delicious," the quest for its meaning begins. Everyone has a different personal definition of the word and war looms. In Activity 2 of the GEMS activities, students in a "scientific convention" often need to define a word, and refine their descriptive language, just as scientists do.

The Slimy Book
by Babette Cole
Red Fox, 2003
Grades: Preschool—4

Lighthearted look at slime of the "sticky, sludgy, slippy, sloppy, ploppy, creepy kind" and where it may be found—around the house, in invertebrate creatures, in foods, and maybe even outer space. Excellent and fun descriptive language of the properties of an intriguing form of matter.

The Three Astronauts
by Umberto Eco; illustrated by Eugenio Carmi
Harcourt Brace Jovanovich, San Diego. 1989
Grades: K—5

An American, a Russian, and a Chinese astronaut take off separately in their own rockets with the goal of being first on Mars. They all land at the same time, immediately distrusting each other. When they encounter a Martian their cultural differences disappear as they unite against him. In a surprise happy ending, they recognize the Martian's kindness toward a baby bird and extend this understanding to differences between all peoples. Younger children may not get the full benefit of the sophisticated illustrations and humor. Unfortunately, the astronauts are all male, with no women characters or references.

The Time Machine and Other Cases: Einstein Anderson, Science Detective
by Seymour Simon
Illustrated by S. D. Schindler
Camelot, 1999
Grades: 4-8

Readers are invited to have fun matching wits with this junior science detective, as he investigates and explains ten mind-boggling mysteries of science--from why his friend's rocket doesn't work to how to speed up slow-moving ketchup. Ketchup is another substance that sometimes acts as a solid and sometimes as a liquid.

The Toothpaste Millionaire
by Jean Merrill; illustrated by Jan Palmer
Houghton Mifflin, Boston. 1972
Grades: 5—8

Incensed by the price of a tube of toothpaste, twelve-year-old Rufus tries making his own from bicarbonate of soda with peppermint or vanilla flavoring. Assisted by his friend Kate and his math class, his company grows to a corporation with stock and bank loans. Beginning on page 47, Rufus designs a machine for filling toothpaste tubes, which is a nice tie-in to the designing spacecraft activities in Activity 3.

The Wise Woman and Her Secret
by Eve Merriam   **(OUT OF PRINT)**
illustrated by Linda Graves
Simon & Schuster, New York. 1991
Grades: K–4/5

A wise woman is sought out by many for her wisdom. They look for the secret of her wisdom in the barn and in her house, but only little Jenny who lags and lingers and loiters and wanders finds it. The wise woman tells her, "The secret of wisdom is to be curious—to take the time to look closely, to use all your senses to see and touch and taste and smell and hear. To keep on wandering and wondering." This book, by a noted woman poet, captures the essence of discovery, student-centered, use-your-senses learning, and, as such, is a good accompaniment to many science and mathematics activities. Although out of print, it may be in school libraries.

REVIEWERS

ARIZONA

Sunset Elementary School, Glendale
Phyllis Shapiro

Cholla Junior High School, Phoenix
Brenda Pierce
Leonard Smith

Desert Foothills Junior High School, Phoenix
Nancy M. Bush
George Casner
Joseph Farrier
E. M. Heward
Stephen H. Kleinz

Desert View Elementary School, Phoenix
Walter C. Hart

Lakeview Elementary School, Phoenix
Sandra Jean Caldwell

Lookout Mountain Elementary School, Phoenix
Carole Dunn

Manzanita Elementary School, Phoenix
Sandra Stanley

Maryland Elementary School, Phoenix
David N. Smith

Moon Mountain Elementary School, Phoenix
Karen Lee

Mountain Sky Junior High School, Phoenix
Flo-Ann Barwick Campbell
C. R. Rogers

Mountain View Elementary School, Phoenix
Roberta Vest

Royal Palm Junior High School, Phoenix
Robert E. Foster, III
Nancy Oliveri

Shaw Butte Elementary School, Phoenix
Cheri Balkenbush
Debbie Baratko

Sunnyslope Elementary School, Phoenix
Don Diller
Susan Jean Parchert

Washington School District, Phoenix
Richard Clark*

CALIFORNIA

Columbus Intermediate School, Berkeley
Dawn Fairbanks
José Franco
Ann Gilbert
Karen E. Gordon
Chiyomi Masuda
Jeannie Osuna-MacIsaac
Judy Suessmeier
Phoebe A. Tanner
Carolyn Willard*

University of California Gifted Program
Marc Tatar

Willard Junior High School, Berkeley
Vana Lee James

Montera Junior High School, Oakland
Richard Adams*
Stanley Fukunaga
Barbara Nagel

Sleepy Hollow Elementary School, Orinda
Margaret Lacrampe
Lin Morehouse*

Piedmont High School, Piedmont
George J. Kodros
Jackson Lay*

Cave Elementary School, Vallejo
Dayle Kerstad*
Neil Nelson
Tina L. Nievelt
Geraldine Piglowski
James Salak
Bonnie Square

Dan Mini Elementary School, Vallejo
Gerald Bettman
James A. Coley*
Jane Erni

Pennycook Elementary School, Vallejo
Lee Cockrum*
Deloris Parker Doster

Kathy Nachbaur Mans
Sandra Rhodes
Aldean Sharp
Robert L. Wood

ILLINOIS

Waubonsie Valley High School, Aurora
Kurt K. Engel
Thomas G. Martinez
Mark Pennington
Sher Renken*
Michael Terronez

Thayer J. Hill Junior High School, Naperville
Sue Atac
Miriam Bieritz
Betty J. Cornell
Athena Digrindakis
Alice W. Dube
Anne Hall
Linda Holdorf
Mardie Krumlauf
Lon Lademann
Mary Lou Lipscomb
Bernadine Lynch
Anne M. Martin
Elizabeth R. Martinez
Judith Mathison
Joan Maute
Peggy E. McCall
Judy Ronaldson

KENTUCKY

Johnson Middle School, Louisville
Martha Ash
Pamela Bayr
Pam Boykin
John Dyer

Mildretta Hinkle
Peggy Madry
Steve Reeves

Knight Middle School, Louisville
Jennifer L. Carson
Susan M. Freepartner
Jacqueline Mayes
Donna J. Stevenson

Museum of History and Science, Louisville
Deborah M. Hornback
Amy S. Lowen*
Dr. William McLean Sudduth*

Newburg Middle School, Louisville
Sue M. Brown
Nancy Hottman*
Brenda W. Logan
Patricia A. Sauer
Janet W. Varon

Rangeland Elementary School, Louisville
Judy Allin
April Bond
Mary Anne Davis
Barbara Hockenbury
Carol Trussell

Robert Frost Middle School, Louisville
Lindagarde Dalton
Tom B. Davidson
Tracey Ferdinand
Rebecca S. Rhodes
Nancy Weber

Stuart Middle School, Louisville
Jane L. Finan
Patricia C. Futch
Nancy L. Hack
Debbie Ostwalt
Gil Polston

MICHIGAN

Bellevue Middle School, Bellevue
Stanley L. Guzy
Sandy Lellis

Lake Michigan Catholic Elementary School, Benton Harbor
Laura Borlik
Joan A. Rybarczyk

F. C. Reed Middle School, Bridgeman
Ronald Collins
Richard Fodor
Betty Meyerink

Buchanan Middle School, Buchanan
Rhea Fitzgerald Noble
Robert Underly

Centreville Junior High School, Centreville
Sandra A. Burnett

Comstock Northeast Middle School, Comstock
Colleen Cole
Karen J. Hileski

Delton-Kellogg Middle School, Delton
Sharon Christensen*

Gull Lake Middle School, Hickory Corners
Gary Denton
Stirling Fenner

The Gagie School, Kalamazoo
Beth Covey
Dr. Alonzo Hannaford
Barbara Hannaford

St. Monica Elementary School, Kalamazoo
John O'Toole

Western Michigan University, Kalamazoo
Dr. Phillip T. Larsen*

Lake Center Elementary School, Portage
Iola Dunsmore
Suzanne Lahti

Portage North Middle School, Portage
John D. Baker
Daniel French

St. Monica Elementary School, Portage
Margaret Erich

NEW YORK

Albert Leonard Junior High School, New Rochelle
Frank Capuzelo
Frank Faraone
Seymour Golden
David Selleck

Barnard School, New Rochelle
Richard Golden*

City School District of New Rochelle, New Rochelle
Dr. John V. Pozzi*

Columbus Elementary School, New Rochelle
Lester Hallerman
Cindy Klein

George M. Davis Elementary School, New Rochelle
Robert Nebens
Charles Yochim

Isaac E. Young Junior High School, New Rochelle
Michael Colasuonno
Vincent Iacovelli
Bruce Zeller

Trinity Elementary School, New Rochelle
Robert Broderick

Ward Elementary School, New Rochelle
Eileen Paolicelli
John Russo

Webster Magnet Elementary School, New Rochelle
Helene Berman
Antoinette DiGuglielmo
Donna MacCrae
Bruce Seiden

Heathcote Elementary School, Scarsdale
Steven Frantz

Scarsdale Junior High School, Scarsdale
Linda Dixon

*Trial test coordinators

~ Notes ~

~ Notes ~

~ Notes ~

~ Notes ~